In *Hope for Your Homeschool*, September extends a compassionate hand to every family educating children at home. With all the wisdom a mother of ten and grandmother of many can possess, September delves into the most common doubts and concerns that cloud the homeschooling journey—questions of adequacy, socialization, personal time, and the overarching fear of whether it's all worth it.

This book is not just a beacon of encouragement, but a transformative tool. She reminds us that we can turn our homeschool from a daunting task to a joyful journey through biblical insights, heartfelt stories, and practical guidance. Her approach helps us see beyond immediate struggles and embrace a vision that's not only about academic excellence but also about shaping hearts and minds for a purposeful life.

September's words remind us that homeschooling is more than an educational choice. It's a journey of faith, love, and profound growth—for us and our kids! She reassures us that, despite the challenges, the rewards of homeschooling are monumental. *Hope for Your Homeschool* is a faith-filled companion to uplift and inspire you to find joy, strength, and, most importantly, hope in your homeschooling adventure.

**TRICIA GOYER**, homeschooling mom of ten and bestselling author of ninety books, including *Homeschool Basics: How to Get Started, Keep Motivated, and Bring Out the Best in Your Kids*

Homeschooling. I've been at it for a long time now, having homeschooled seven kids over twenty-four years—and as a veteran homeschool mom, I can tell you that this is the book I wish I had read when we first started homeschooling. Drawing from decades of experience, September points new homeschool parents back to the *reason* they made such a monumental decision and reminds veterans that the journey is worth finishing well. Whether you need encouragement to stay the course, practical advice, or a hand to hold as you embrace homeschooling your children, this book is for you.

**HEIDI ST. JOHN,** bestselling author of the Becoming MomStrong series; speaker and founder of Faith That Speaks

*Hope for Your Homeschool* is more than a guide; it's a deep well of encouragement that will renew your spirit, refocus your purpose, and remind you to embrace and treasure every step of your homeschooling journey.

**GINGER HUBBARD,** bestselling author of *Don't Make Me Count to Three* and *I Can't Believe You Just Said That*; cohost of the podcast *Parenting with Ginger Hubbard*

In *Hope for Your Homeschool,* mom of ten September McCarthy gently guides us through the transformative journey of homeschooling. This book isn't just about teaching with confidence; it's a heartfelt exploration of cultivating relationships, fostering hope, and simplifying the educational path. This book is an essential resource for anyone seeking a profound vision for homeschooling that goes beyond textbooks, emphasizing the essence of family and the joy of learning together. *Hope for Your Homeschool* will help you nurture a home filled with love, purpose, and the promise of a brighter future.

**JENNIFER PEPITO,** founder of The Peaceful Press

*Hope for Your Homeschool* is everything this generation of home educators needs: it is practical, yet peaceful; challenging, but encouraging; a call to excellence, but not at the cost of relationship. Whether you are at the beginning of your homeschool journey or have been at it for decades, there is something in September's book to resonate with you. Home education can only improve because this book is in the world.

**PHYLICIA MASONHEIMER,** founder and CEO of Every Woman a Theologian

September McCarthy's *Hope for Your Homeschool* is not just a guide—it's a lifeline for overwhelmed homeschoolers. Learn to navigate the pitfalls of overload, comparison, and defeat with wisdom and grace. Discover the transformative power of prioritizing relationships and giving yourself space to grow. Face your fears head-on and manage expectations with confidence. With McCarthy's compassionate insight, homeschooling isn't just an educational journey—it's a journey of discovery, resilience, and unshakable joy.

**GINNY YURICH,** bestselling author of *Until the Streetlights Come On*; host of the *1000 Hours Outside Podcast*; founder of 1000 Hours Outside

# HOPE

## for your

# HOMESCHOOL

- - - - - - - - - - - - -

Start strong,
stay the course,
& finish with
**JOY**

- - - - - - - - - - - - -

# September McCarthy

**MOODY PUBLISHERS**
CHICAGO

Edited by Amanda Cleary Eastep
Interior design: Brandi Davis
Cover design: Kaylee Lockenour Dunn
Cover vector of children silhouettes copyright © 2024 by majivecha/Adobe Stock (63461045). All rights reserved. Cover vector of graduates silhouette copyright © 2024 by Adopik/VectorStock (43626868). All rights reserved.
Author photo: Emilee Carpenter

Library of Congress Cataloging-in-Publication Data

Names: McCarthy, September, author.
Title: Hope for your homeschool : start strong, stay the course, and finish
  with joy / September McCarthy.
Description: Chicago, IL : Moody Publishers, 2024. | Includes
  bibliographical references. | Summary: "You weren't meant to do this on
  your own. Whether it's day one or year ten of your homeschooling
  journey, you can draw from this well of wisdom and encouragement!
  McCarthy helps create a culture at home that fortifies hearts and
  sharpens young minds"-- Provided by publisher.
Identifiers: LCCN 2023057259 (print) | LCCN 2023057260 (ebook) | ISBN
  9780802433732 (paperback) | ISBN 9780802471130 (ebook)
Subjects: LCSH: Home schooling. | Motivation in education. | BISAC:
  RELIGION / Christian Education / Children & Youth | RELIGION / Christian
  Education / General
Classification: LCC LC40 .M42 2024  (print) | LCC LC40 (ebook) | DDC
  371.01/2--dc23/eng/20231221
LC record available at https://lccn.loc.gov/2023057259
LC ebook record available at https://lccn.loc.gov/2023057260

Originally delivered by fleets of horse-drawn wagons, the affordable paperbacks from D. L. Moody's publishing house resourced the church and served everyday people. Now, after more than 125 years of publishing and ministry, Moody Publishers' mission remains the same— even if our delivery systems have changed a bit. For more information on other books (and resources) created from a biblical perspective, go to www.moodypublishers.com or write to:

Moody Publishers
820 N. LaSalle Boulevard
Chicago, IL 60610

1 3 5 7 9 10 8 6 4 2

*Printed in the United States of America*

To my ten children,

Our homeschool journey has changed my life.

I am passing the baton to you now.

Run with perseverance and faithfulness.

You are my magnum opus.

# Contents

**PART THREE: FINISH WITH JOY**

# Introduction

You were brave to show up here and seek encouragement and hope. More extraordinarily, you were brave to say yes to the decision to homeschool. We all know the world doesn't come knocking on your door with a morning coffee mixed with a word of encouragement, and your children are not jumping out of bed and running to the schoolroom every morning to greet you with excited cheers before the day begins. At least not every day. Homeschooling can be lonely and amazing, all at the same time. In the loneliest of moments, when we're unsure of our purpose, weary of the journey, or need the motivation to keep going and to finish strong, we all could use another voice or word of hope to stay the course.

This book is one such place. Step back from the swirling motion of life—pencils scratching on paper, minds mulling over math facts. Close the day planner, take a deep breath, and let someone else speak life and hope into your day because we know that what we do in our quiet spaces affects every part of our home and school.

For those just beginning their homeschooling journey, here you will find a clear call to purpose and the tools you need to start strong. Each part of this book will cheer you on to stay the course and give you the hope and help you need to finish with joy.

When I think back to our homeschool beginnings, I remember all the victories and insecurities. Oh, the insecurities! For almost thirty years, I have been homeschooling our ten children, the youngest and oldest having an age span of eighteen years between them. This means I will have been homeschooling for four decades before we graduate our last homeschooled child.

Decades of experience and life-changing lessons will be shared with you on these pages. I hope you will hold tightly to the rope I am throwing to you. It will be a lifeline in the days and years to follow.

You are the best person to homeschool your children, and your journey will look different than anyone else's. Remind yourself of this when you are faced with doubt and insecurity. Because, let's be honest, you will be.

Every time you pick up this book and turn a page, it is my hope you will find a truth that speaks to you, knowing I have walked this road for three decades now and will be cheering you on through each chapter. This book will be a timeless treasure of hope and help to the homeschooler in any and every season. You'll notice in the table of contents that the book is divided into three parts. Part One will propel you to take the steps from your decision to homeschool to start strong and live out a plan and purpose daily. You will find helpful tools to creating great daily rhythms. Part Two will help you stay on course and keep your focus. Time and experience will grow your confidence, but here you will find hope for the perseverance needed to show up every day. Part Three will carry you to the finish line.

At the end of each chapter, you'll find four sections that will guide you to consider areas of growth and reflection for your home and school:

**Personal Reflection** summarizes the chapter emphasis and will help you consider how your homeschooling can change or improve. Consider this as a homeschool health check.

**Personal Challenge** asks questions and helps you walk out the steps to a better homeschool journey.

**Drawing from the Well:** At the end of each chapter, we will gather at "the well." This is your space to drink from "rivers of living water" (John 7:38). When we come to the well, we approach with empty and receiving hands, an open heart, and a thirsty soul, waiting to be refreshed by the Word of God and the wisdom He offers—the wellspring of life that never runs dry.

**A Prayer for My Homeschool:** This is a short prayer you can say or use to guide you in your own prayers.

You can do this. You are doing this. You can homeschool with hope because you are not alone.

*part one*

# Start Strong

"**God** chose you for this task,
so **d**on't question **H**is ability
to choose wisely."[1]

**JAMIE ERICKSON**

1. Jamie Erickson, *Homeschool Bravely: How to Squash Doubt, Trust God, and Teach Your Child with Confidence* (Chicago: Moody, 2019), 47.

- - • •• •• • •• •• • • • ••• •

# chapter 1

# Where Do I Begin?

*N*ot all of us will feel "called" to homeschool. Your beginnings may not be marked by warm and fuzzy feelings, and you may not have a carefully laid out plan or a big support system. I have learned that although all beginnings are different, there is hope in homeschooling for us all. Whether you are just beginning or are at the start of another year of homeschooling, you have purposed to do it well. This is all that really matters. My story isn't yours, but I hope my beginnings will inspire you to start strong and stay the course.

Our first day of homeschooling will always be my favorite memory in this journey. What is so amazing is that I don't re-member experiencing fear, nervousness, indecision, or worry. What we *did* have that day were two used wooden school desks set in the corner of an end room in the trailer we were renting at the time; a simple chalkboard hung on the wall; and an excited "showing up" on our first day of school.

I had started with a dream to homeschool my children. The early years of parenting afforded me the time and an awareness that what my children learned now would affect their future. With a vision to teach my children in the way they each learned uniquely, I had a purpose to be their primary teacher in life and learning. My dream, my vision, and my purpose propelled me to the end of each year since and served as the pillars of my schedules, my curriculum, my expectations, and my focus from the moment I woke up.

My two kids didn't know homeschooling was all new to me. They never asked me if I had a degree or which curriculum we would be using each year. We just began, used what we had, and enjoyed our time together. Our family created a lifestyle of learning. I asked others for help and wisdom and asked Jesus to guide us every single moment. Literally.

*Homeschooling may be the hardest job you will ever love.*

I am sure you didn't make this decision lightly. Homeschooling is a big decision, and you are most likely feeling the weight, worry, doubt, and concern that *maybe* it wasn't the right decision for you or your family. This decision also comes with excitement, anticipation, and fun! Homeschooling decisions are different for everyone. Most likely you made this decision for your family and didn't really take yourself into consideration when you said yes to homeschooling. Now you are wondering where to begin, looking around at what everyone else is doing, and making the best plans for the best education for your children.

What is the first thing that comes to your mind when you hear this question about homeschooling: "Where do I begin?" Do you think of a homeschool space and how to set it up? How to choose curriculum or set schedules? Maybe you wonder who to talk to and what the advantages and disadvantages of homeschooling are. Whether this is your first rodeo, or you've been in this for a while, the same questions apply. We don't always need to re-create the wheel, especially when something is working; but every summer, we all should and need to ask ourselves, "Where do I begin?"

Always begin with your *why*. Remembering *why* you chose this path will inform your *how*. My beginnings were marked with the purpose to redeem every minute I had with my children as they were growing up. I purposed to teach them those things I believed to be the most important. I knew I didn't want the world and its influences to have first dibs on their heart. I wanted to help my children thrive in their schoolwork and not feel like a number waiting for help. I chose to homeschool to show them God's faithfulness in the little and big things of life. I didn't choose to homeschool my children because I was prepared or had it all figured out. I chose to homeschool because I knew why I wanted to, and in some ways, felt deep down that I needed to.

Let's take a deep breath here. Even if you have a clearer idea of your why, you'll still have doubts. Consider the list below:

- You may be a confident person, but homeschooling scares you.
- You may not be a worrier, but homeschooling has you a little (or a lot) stressed.
- You may not consider yourself a teacher, but now you feel the pressure to "become something you are not."

When doubt creeps into the cracks of my calling and my convictions, I have learned to stop, step back, consider, remember, and remind myself of the following: there is a bigger picture than what is before me right now.

Now read the sentence below aloud:

*I am a significant small piece of God's larger plan.*

There will be more fruit and reward than the hardest part of this right in front of us. We just can't see it yet. However, we can put our trust in the Creator of all things good and right and perfect, who has us on His mind and always held in His hands. He holds creation in His power and plan every day, so why does this one thing seem to be too big right now? We aren't invincible and how we do in this decision and how we get through this journey matters just as much as our children's education.

Our homeschooling *why* will grow as we go. It may feel weak and full of the unknown today, but someday, we will look back and see the reward. We trust the process because God knows the end before we begin, and we place our trust and confidence daily in His care and provision.

## CREATE A WHY VISION AND STATEMENT

Casting your doubts aside and resting in the assurance that your abilities and confidence will grow with you as you go is your first step to creating a strong vision that will last. I have been homeschooling for three decades, and the vision I had from the beginning has not only sustained me but has come full circle with more blessings than I could have ever imagined.

There may be a lot of voices, or even feelings of fear, that have propelled you to choose homeschooling for you and your family. When you are in the middle of your longest days of homeschooling, those people, opinions, and emotions will not sustain you. Take time to consider the *who* you are homeschooling and the *how* this will look for your family.

Even better, start with the answers to *why* questions like these:

Do you see amazing opportunities to spend more time with your children,
... to grow closer as a family,
... to teach them uniquely and diligently in the way they should go?

Can you see the possibilities to give them more one-on-one time on focus areas,
... to come alongside them in their struggles,
... to grow their gifts and to walk with them in their relationship with the Lord?

Having a why vision and statement can help keep you rooted and grounded when days are hard.

Read the section below, adapted from Deuteronomy 6:5–9, and consider your vision and purpose in homeschooling based on the highlighted bullet points below. It is with His wisdom and guidance we can find excitement and hope for the mornings we rise and are weary or face obstacles along the way. These verses are a wonderful model for your homeschooling and can be a placeholder for the days when you may lose sight of your vision.

*"Love the L*ORD *your God with all your heart and with all your soul and with all your strength. These commandments that I give you today are to be on your hearts. Impress them on your children. Talk about them when you sit at home and when you walk along the road, when you lie down and when you get up."*
Deuteronomy 6:5–9 (NIV)

*"Love the L*ORD *your God with all your heart"*

- Devotion is the best way to sum up the first part of this verse from Deuteronomy. There is no doubt I love my children. If I have been called to homeschool, then my devotion to God and my children are my priorities.
- God called me to homeschooling and will be with me through every step.
- When God calls me to something, He loves me enough to equip me for what is before me.
- God has my whole heart and not just the pieces or parts that are comfortable and easy; He will grow me and strengthen me as we do this together.
- Am I making time for God on a personal level? Does my relationship with Him reflect His love in my life and home?
- Homeschooling will give me more time to model godliness and teach my children about God and His character, attributes, and truths.
- How will I live this out in my homeschooling?
- How can I learn more about God's love and learn about Him in my homeschooling?

*"And with all your soul"*

- How do I homeschool my children when I am weary and tired?
- He has provided me with prayer, worship, communion, and time to refresh my soul.
- Loving God with all my soul will restore and refresh me in lonely moments.
- Homeschooling doesn't have to be a dry and barren land where we are forgotten, and our souls are desperate and weary.
- He sustains us in all we do for Him.
- I can direct my homeschooling prayers and petitions to the Lord of my life, just as in any other area.
- A satisfied soul can overflow into my homeschool.

*"And with all your strength"*

- Rather than considering time with God and building a relationship as extra things to "fit in," I can remember this is the closest and most dear relationship I will have.
- My time and devotion in knowing God's love will transfer into my homeschooling as I model and teach my children His example.
- When we serve too many masters, our devotion is spread thin. Homeschooling to grow and strengthen our family's love for God is a "why" I cannot ignore. We all will reap fruit in abundance.

*"These commandments that **I** give you today are to be on your hearts"*

- As my heart receives His commands, I will walk in His ways daily.
- When I recognize something of value, I invest in it. There is no greater reward than to train my children to love the Lord with all their heart, soul, and strength (and mind).

*"**I**mpress them on your children"*

This part of the verse requires action as you take opportunities throughout your homeschool day.

There were so many nights I would lie awake while my household slept, and I wondered if I really taught my children anything worth remembering that day. I would recall the moments of bringing God's truth to the breakfast table. I would choose verses and a focus for the day, that we would keep before us. When the kids had conflicts over who was going to practice the piano first, or complaining about how long their schoolwork was taking, I would take the time to stop the bookwork and the busywork and "impress on their hearts" God's command and example for us to love one another. We'd talk about diligence and good stewardship of what God had given us. I'd remind them of our daily verse, our focus, and gently usher our day back into a good momentum.

As I looked back on my days, I could see where virtue was impressed upon our lives in the most mundane moments. Amid whining, arguing, laziness, or sharing, God's Word was at the center of our discussions and, most importantly, our solutions. Consistently talking and teaching throughout daily activities left an impression on my children's hearts that I will never regret taking time for.

When you imagine the action of impressing God's command-ments onto your children's hearts, the choice to homeschool is an open book, and your daily investment, time, and teaching are like the folded pages and consistency in learning. You are living out His commandments and His precepts and showing your children how to walk in His way daily.

What an opportunity God has given us with our choice to home-school. Redeem the time and the season, and remember His love endures forever.

### *"Talk about them when you sit at home"*

You will have many opportunities to talk to your children about the Lord's faithfulness as you homeschool. We don't home-school because we are Christians; but because we are Christians, we use our homeschooling time at home to have conversations, read the Word, and ask the hard questions that encourage deeper discussion than the dinner table conversations about sports. Part of my "why" was to impact the hearts of my children before the world could. With the time we have had at home, we navigated their choices, their friendships, their identity and sexuality, and their future pursuits, all through the lens of God's Word and His wisdom. The hours are opportunities, and we often forget the value our communication has as an impact on our child's faith. We can weave Christ's teachings into our all our daily interac-tions. It isn't enough to be a Christian family and assume our kids will love God.

*"And when you walk along the road"*

One of my children struggled with learning, and my choice to homeschool her meant that I was able to show up to help her work through her schoolwork with patience and perseverance, but to also be present for the tears and frustration daily as well. It is easier to show up with solutions to a math or reading problem than it is to be committed to matters of the heart. Because we were homeschooling, I was able to see what was going on in her heart, beneath the surface.

It was a rare gift to show up every day with a truth from God's Word to bring light to the situation and to help her focus on His precepts daily. I reminded her of His love for her. I was present when she got discouraged and wanted to give up. I shared about her value and worth and the gift of His love to us when we least feel like loving the hard parts of us. We had so many moving parts to our days, and I discovered the opportunities were endless when it came to impressing His commands and love on the hearts of my children.

Whether while reading, teaching, driving, or correcting papers, every homeschooling moment is an opportunity to share the love of Jesus with your children. He affords us so many hours, days, and years with them, and every one matters.

*"When you lie down and when you get up"*

Every morning, before diving headlong into a stack of books and routine, I discovered a formative and sustaining rhythm I practiced over the years that has stayed with my children even when other things did not. My former structured approach to most things in life would have dictated a strict schedule to begin with our bookwork after morning chores and breakfast. I found a smooth transition from breakfast to our schoolwork with a time of worship.

We began each morning with a slow roll into the living room, gathering on couches with babies on my lap, Bibles, a basket of books, verse cards, character-based learning materials, and hands-on and interactive supplements at my disposal. Often, my Sunday evening prep times would begin with a reflection of our previous week and the areas we seemed to be struggling in the most. I would choose a topic or a focus for the new week that would bring everything we do back God's Word. For example, if there had been a lot of whining and complaining, I would pick out verses and stories that focused on gratefulness; then I'd incorporate solutions into our days to combat and cure the whining. When we struggled with laziness and defeat, I would lay out a plan with a focus on the character quality of perseverance and diligence.

These Sunday evening preparation times allowed our homeschooling to be filled with intentional moments of character growth and solutions for us to work on together. We read and learned together. We sang and talked and prayed for one another. As we moved from this to our schoolwork, we had a focus to keep before us, and it allowed me to pause to refocus as needed.

You have been called to so much more than educating your children. In fact, that is the most exciting part of the purpose you have before you. Don't let the weight of the task thwart your efforts. It will come to you. You will find the moments to impress the most important things on their hearts—as you seek Him and seize the opportunities.

## CONSIDER YOUR CALLING

Your calling will only last as long as your purpose holds its place in your life. Your goals will determine how you move forward, so now is the time to consider your calling and determine your next steps. If you want to start strong, remember God knows the details and has promised to provide for us as we draw near to Him.

You know your family better than anyone and what they need in this time. Don't wait for the perfect scenario and a completed checklist before taking the steps to begin. Be careful to watch the heart of your home as you start. It may be easy to get caught up in the roles, the defined purpose, and the checklists and forget to hold on to the joy in the process.

Your homeschool will only be as strong as the anchor to which you tie your vision and purpose. Keep Him central to all that you choose to do and commit your ways to Him. When you rise in the morning, let your lips speak words of need and praise. When you show up for your family, show them the passion and purpose God has called you to by leading in love and the fruit of His Spirit. As you end your day, pour out your needs, tears, praise, and prayer to a God who has called you to a greater purpose than even you can see in this moment. The best is yet to come.

······· *personal reflection* ·······

What are my greatest concerns or stumbling blocks to beginning with confidence and peace?

How can I start strong?

······· *personal challenge* ·······

Today, I will replace my doubts and worries with confidence in knowing that all good things begin with small steps of saying yes to the Lord and allowing Him to lead me with wisdom and peace.

Today, I will choose to see the areas that are hard in homeschooling as something I can control, rather than allow them to control me. I will reap the fruit of perseverance. Not every list is a "must do" or checklist, but rather a guide to give me steps to grow in hope as I homeschool.

Here is my mini pep talk to help you stay focused on the here and now. Don't get too ahead of yourself. Take a few moments to consider the following thoughts that will help you start strong.

1. Choose your homeschool style. What fits your family the best?
2. Plan to be consistent, dedicated to great learning and a balanced home and schedule.
3. Discover your own strengths and your weaker areas and plan accordingly.
4. Set your end of year goals and work backward.
5. Find a community. Find your people.
6. Give yourself (and your children) grace to begin.
7. Show up daily and stay committed.
8. Take a deep breath and know your purpose every day.
9. Pick your start day and make it special!

*········ drawing from the well ········*

Jesus doesn't expect us to come to the well prepared or polished. He is waiting for us expectantly because we all need to be reminded that we are not homeschooling alone, and His words can refresh and restore our souls.

*"And the LORD will guide you continually and satisfy your desire in scorched places and make your bones strong; and you shall be like a watered garden, like a spring of water, whose waters do not fail."*
Isaiah 58:11

*"Come to me, all you who are weary and burdened, and I will give you rest. Take my yoke upon you and learn from me, for I am gentle and humble in heart, and you will find rest for your souls."*
Matthew 11:28–29 NIV

*···· a prayer for my homeschool ····*

Father God, help me to choose to not allow hard things to control me, my decisions, and my reactions. I give You my homeschool and ask for clarity and purpose that aligns with Your will for our lives. I trust You to replace my doubts and worries with confidence as I surrender today to You. In Jesus' name, Amen.

*chapter 2*

- - • • • • • • • • • • • •

# The Mistakes I Will Make

*P*lease sit up and write your spelling words in print and cursive, so we can all have lunch."

No movement.

"Did you hear me?"

With her forehead resting on the palm of her hand, her elbows propped up on the table, her shoulders slumped, and her pencil "obediently" scratching out the neatly written words on repeat, I recognized my daughter's mood. It wasn't the grumpy, hard-to-get-along-with, I-don't-want-to-do-this mood. My eyes were well trained now. My heart had been conditioned, and my homeschool antenna was picking up the signals loud and clear. My daughter (along with my other children) was disengaged and struggling to stay focused. Every little task had become insurmountable for all of them.

Oh, the mistakes we will make. In this chapter, I share some of the most common mistakes we will make in homeschooling and how to remedy them. Mistakes are not bad if we learn from them, but it is better to have the foresight and knowledge of the potential ahead to help us avoid them. Learn from me and let my mistakes help you.

## MISTAKE #1: OVERLOAD

Number one on my list of the mistakes I have made as a homeschooler is the habit of overloading assignments and activities to an already crowded schedule. This is one of the most common mistakes when starting homeschooling. By being aware and having a humble heart, we can quickly recognize the tell-tale signs and reset when the symptoms of overload begin to show up.

Starting strong is the goal, but starting *too* strong can overwhelm and overtake you and your family. This can also be called "too much, too soon." The eagerness and desire to "succeed" when we begin homeschooling can sneak up on us in ways we don't expect unless we acknowledge from the start that we *will* make mistakes. When we fail to identify the warning signs, admit the mistakes, apologize, and change the trajectory, we may get ourselves stuck in a pattern of frustration and overwhelm.

Let me share a secret with you. The three little big words "I am sorry" will be a reset on all your personal homeschool mistakes that cannot be fixed with a simple eraser. There may be days you overwhelm your children with too much work or forget the importance of rest. Don't get me wrong, your kiddos will make their own mistakes, and you will feel like your red pen and your principal role will be overworked and underpaid on many a day. But, for the mistakes you repeat, a humble and heartfelt apology will go a long way. Give yourself a gold star if you preemptively recognize these patterns before they become problems.

To the best of your ability, expect and plan for mistakes and be prepared to own your part in pivoting where you can. Otherwise, your homeschool will be filled with a lot of correcting and not a lot of productive learning. Overcompensation and overload are often symptoms of fear of failure. We strive to fit it all in and make sure our children are getting enough in an attempt to achieve a level of success that is actually unnecessary or unattainable. In the end, we are left with kiddos who are burned out, stressed out, and checked out.

Staying aware of how our children are pacing in their work and adapting to new concepts will help you avoid the meltdown and overwhelm we often miss in our children in an attempt to "get it all done." It's our job to have eyes on what is working and what is not. Watch for signs of weariness in your children. Examine your schedules to discern where you have expected too much in one day. Engaging on levels of awareness and sensitivity to your child is vital. Study the patterns of your homeschool. Finding a balance is key for all of you.

I have found some of my greatest homeschool victories on the heels of my mistakes. When one of my children struggled with a hefty and long reading assignment I'd given, I made the pivot to allow them to listen to an audiobook version while tracking with the printed reading material with a highlighter. When memorization of math facts was a tipping point for tears after I'd pressed in and required more practice, I changed course and helped them learn math facts through action steps and rhymes. I then watched as relief washed away their defeat.

There is nothing like the reward of seeing the light come back on in your child's countenance and reengagement after we pay close attention to what is working and what is not and pivot. Our mistakes can become our victories, and our losses will turn into wins. One day we make a mistake and the next day we recognize the pattern and tell-tale signs before our homeschooling hits "distress mode." We then take a detour to avert the crisis and can celebrate the victory. Mistakes are opportunities to learn and grow. Don't get stuck in the discouragement of not doing everything right the first time, and most of all, celebrate your wins.

### How to Avoid Overload

The following ideas are certainly not an exhaustive list but will apply in general to avoiding overwhelm in your schedule. After reading through the bulleted list, I recommend filling in the blank lines with specific areas that come to mind as you evaluate how your homeschooling is going. Identify the warning signs you are beginning to notice and ask questions that will help you trouble-shoot solutions.

- Create your schedule with a lot of wiggle room and break time (fun and rest).
- Save the lofty goals and expectations for later.
- Space out lessons and rotate subjects by day or semester.
- Save grading for your weekend.
- Discern between overload and laziness.
- Maximize teaching and learning by combining ages/grade levels for select subjects.
- Choose a minimal curriculum.
- Adjust assignments to pull out key learning and skip redundancy.
- Get *your* rest.

- Break up your day and schedule to include free time and healthy habits (exercise, quiet time, a simple walk, a phone call with a friend or loved one, lunch with your spouse, playdates).
- Don't overcommit to extracurricular activities that overfill your schedule.
- Review difficult learning areas individually to avoid frustration and discouragement.
- Be consistent with getting the work done.
- Work ahead when and where you can without too much strain to allow for more time in other areas.
- Make a printed schedule for each child to follow.

Every day, we struggle with _____.

I find my family complaining the most about _____.

I don't know how to help my child with _____.

We seem to be doing a lot of schoolwork and not enough _____

_____.

I am overwhelmed regularly by _____.

Homeschooling is not what I thought it would be because ____

_____.

## MISTAKE #2: COMPARISON VS. WISDOM

Every day for one full school year I sat with a myriad of reading tools, books, flashcards, and my third-born while the house was quiet and the littles were napping. This was our designated one-on-one time to practice his reading. I was worried and wondered,

*Shouldn't he be reading by now?* He was as smart as a whip. He was clever, and his ingenuity and analytical skills were through the roof. All my friends who had children the same age were checking out lengthy fiction, biographies, and chapter books from the library for their kids. What was I doing wrong?

I had pretty much overcome my insecurity about my ability to teach a child to read. It is a milestone most homeschool parents worry about reaching from the start, and I won't pretend that I didn't worry too. But this was my third new-to-reading homeschool student. We had a strong phonics base, and we practiced every day, but each time we sat down to read, we were met with challenges. Was I missing something? Did I miss a step, did I not spend enough time teaching him, or did I miss a significant learning concern in his schooling?

Now looking back, it seems so minor, but it was a big deal to me at the time. And after much reflection, I realized most of my worry and fears came from comparing him to other kids "his age." A loving and wise friend a few years ahead of me in this journey told me to be patient and not press it. She encouraged me to stay focused and consistent, but not to fear. Then, the summer before third grade rolled around, I started to find him reading on his own—up in the branches of a tree with chapter books, under his covers with a flashlight, and checking out books at the library I never thought he would read.

It was like turning on a light switch. Between our homeschool groundwork and his personal development, it just seemed to click one day. Although his independent reading happened later than I expected, he became a strong reader, his ability and pace

now surpassing others his age. His interests, curiosity, and ingenuity drove his desire to find answers and solutions, and experience adventures in those books. He became a strong reader, and
I became more confident in trusting my groundwork to meet my
children's personal development when it was time.

I had minimized all the work we had been doing and doubting
every inch of the process. When I questioned my son's progress
and pressed in for faster results, I instilled doubt in him and cast
a shadow on what had been a special time we had together with
books, words, adventures, and his love for those things. When I
listened to wisdom from a caring friend, it made a difference. It
changed my perspective and allowed me to see the truth behind
the little wall of comparisons I had erected around this situation.

*Comparison blinds us to the beauty and truth God has placed*
*right in front of us, and wisdom helps us uncover a new way*
*of seeing and beholding the truth.*

Twenty-eight years ago, homeschool conventions were new
and shiny and there were only a few select vendors and speakers.
We were pioneers as conference attendees, with fewer choices and
a narrower mindset. This world has grown exponentially and the
selection and choices available to homeschoolers now are beyond
what we can fathom when we first enter the wide convention hall
doors. Even the most confident and focused homeschooler can't
help but get caught up in the overwhelming activity and feeling
that they aren't doing enough.

The internet has grown to be a homeschooling comparison

trap. We make the mistake (there's that word again) of not just looking, inquiring, researching, and finding what is best, but allowing our minds to drift and compare and to unconsciously demean and devalue our own choices. Sadly, doing so undermines the progress and abilities of our own children.

Comparison is the thief of joy. We've heard this on repeat. It won't surprise you to know that this is one of the top three mistakes we all may make as homeschoolers. Oh, we don't think we are comparing, but trust me, it happens every day, in the smallest and biggest of ways.

Social media shines a light on homeschool spaces and favorite curriculums. Speakers share one way that is the "only way," and we sit down with our newly purchased curriculum, doubt written over every penny spent. We carry comparison deeply in the homeschool world because we naturally want the best for our kids. The outcome becomes the ultimate goal rather than what is before us daily.

Conferences, influencers, speakers, and even authors (wink, wink) have a lot to share and offer. I like to gather and sift as I read, shop, look, and follow others. The sifting part is where we either fall into the comparison mindset that leads to doubt and insecurities or lean into wisdom and discernment.

Comparison is sneaky and can inch its way under the cracks of your front door and into your homeschool space with subtle words, doubt, and lack of vision. It can work its way to the core of who you are a homeschool parent, the success in which you measure your child's intelligence or progress, your curriculum choices, and sometimes, your very decision whether to homeschool.

When I took a head-to-toe inventory of my homeschooling, I was able to see the facts for what they were. I recognized patterns that were turning into problems. I took note of the small wins that led to bigger victories. Taking an inventory enabled me to see the whole picture and not focus on the perceived lack that came from comparing small areas of our homeschooling to others. I was able to discern more clearly through an objective lens, which is what I know to be true about my family, God's truths and promises for me (us), and the best tool of discernment: wisdom. I asked for advice, I took my concerns to God in prayer, and I changed the things I needed to change and continued in the rest.

Wisdom is hard-won and is the key to unlocking freedom in the homeschool journey. Wisdom is based on truth and discerning what is best for you and your family. Wisdom offers us freedom from our attempt to control and manage an outcome. Wisdom gives us the tools to make learning less worrisome and more enjoyable and helps us find new solutions to hard problems. Wisdom releases us from the burden of doing it all on our own and shines bright on the gift homeschooling was to us before we began comparing every little thing with the shiny thing next door.

## Squashing Comparison with Wisdom

When I find myself swirling in patterns of defeat, comparison, and overachieving, I ask myself the following questions to squash doubt. We all make mistakes, but wisdom sets us free from the entanglement of living those mistakes on repeat. Consider the questions below and fill in the blanks with your own responses. This will give you an accurate baseline account of how you are doing in the area of comparison.

Do I find myself continually scouring the internet and asking friends for the best curriculum and resources?

Have I changed our homeschooling materials and schedules frequently in the past few years?

Do I believe I am equipped to homeschool my children?

I struggle to be content with _____.

I want my homeschooling to look like _____.

## MISTAKE #3: DEFEAT

How can I say this gently? At some point, you will feel defeated and want to give up. Maybe you've experienced a few rough consecutive weeks (not just days) in your homeschool spaces. No one seems to be learning or listening; your home is falling apart at the seams while you try to hold everything together. You cannot remember the last time your kids showed initiative, learned something new, or showed up with a cheerful spirit. You are done. You've spoken the words that eventually come from every defeated homeschooling parent's mouth: "Would you like to ride the bus and go to public school?" You start believing the lie that you can't show up and keep doing this. These are all signs that certain areas in your home and school need to be addressed.

After a string of mid-morning disruptions in my homeschool, I began to recognize a pattern. Our morning wasn't starting on time, no one seemed to be listening, the teens strolled into the schoolroom late, and nothing seemed to be in its place. I couldn't find my teacher's manual, the ten-year-old "somehow lost" their spelling notebook, and by the time we were engaged in our actual schoolwork, it was time for the baby to take a nap. All momentum I had was lost.

This went the same way every single day. I would go from holding it together, pivoting as needed, teaching through the obstacles, and then it would happen—someone would complain or stop trying. This was always my "last straw." My thoughts would go to defeat: *If they are going to stop trying, then what am I doing here?* And so it went. I would raise my white flag and send everyone to their rooms. I wanted to give up on the whole thing. I wanted to resign from homeschooling, not from my kids.

Defeat is giving up on yourself and your kids. Defeat is throwing up your hands and throwing in the towel. Instead, you can change course, take a break, outsource, or take a step back. That is not defeat. You will make changes in your schedules, your plans, your curriculum, or perhaps your whole approach, but this is not defeat. Give yourself permission to change your mind, see things differently, or set a short-term goal. You are in control of your responses to victories and challenges in your homeschool. Homeschooling does not have to control you.

Digging into the roots of our feelings of defeat will help us identify what is happening below the surface of these feelings of doubt. We may find ourselves creating a false narrative we begin to believe. Those thoughts or lies begin to form our defining takeaways on our homeschooling experiences and lead us to defeat.

*How to Identify and Overcome Defeat*

Defeat can sneak its way into your homeschooling, so it is helpful to learn to identify and squash the symptoms as soon as you can. The list below will help you recognize your concerns and consider solutions, rather than giving up. As you read this list, make note of the moments and thoughts you identify with. This list will give you the clear thinking you need to overcome defeat.

- Don't blame homeschooling for everything that doesn't seem to be working.
- Don't allow worry to become the filter through which you process your homeschooling feelings. Consider your concerns as a tool for finding new solutions.
- Adjust the areas you are finding the most concerning.
- Ask a trusted friend or your spouse to help you evaluate your concerns.
- Identify burnout and make changes to your personal schedule; give yourself space and grace.
- You're not perfect. Don't expect your homeschooling to be.
- Stop making homeschooling something you "do," and make it a lifestyle of learning.
- Remember how equipped you truly are. You know your child better than anyone.

Gospel truth alone saves us from endlessly striving and from the fear, worry, and anxiety triggered by wondering if we (and our homeschools) are enough. The cross of Christ took away our need to work to perfection. The saving power of Jesus' story weaves a new story through the generations of people fleeing from the bondage of slavery, sin, control, and fear. His story changed every-thing. We don't have to worry whether we are "doing enough" to make a difference, or love under the burden of being the perfect mom or homeschooler. The gospel message we choose for our lives is sanctifying, and He redeems all of our mistakes along the way. We have nothing to prove. Christ took the striving away and just asks us to abide. And what a relief it is to meet Him in the very place He is waiting for us.

###### ⋯⋯ *personal reflection* ⋯⋯

Where have I chosen fear, comparison, and overload in our homeschooling journey?

Have I allowed the overwhelming sense of urgency or choices to dictate our plan and purpose?

###### ⋯⋯ *personal challenge* ⋯⋯

I will take time to reevaluate mistakes I may have overlooked or reasoned into my homeschooling mindset. I will show up with humility and listen to wisdom and discernment as we move forward in our homeschooling.

###### ⋯⋯ *drawing from the well* ⋯⋯

I will **repent** of constant striving.

I will **relish** the joy of learning.

I will **rest** in the work of Christ on my behalf.

*"Come to me, all you who are weary and burdened, and I will give you rest. Take my yoke upon you and learn from me, for I am gentle and humble in heart, and you will find rest for your souls."*
Matthew 11:28–29 NIV

###### ⋯ *a prayer for my homeschool* ⋯

Lord, thank You for granting me the opportunity for humility. The opportunity to recognize I am weak, I am not able, I am not as prepared as I wanted to be—but my duty is not success, but faithfulness. Give me the humility to admit my weaknesses and allow You to give me the strength to overcome my insecurities and inabilities. Your faithfulness is a gift, and I rejoice in knowing You are working in and through me. In Jesus' name, Amen.

*chapter 3*

························

# Don't Sacrifice
# Relationships for Roles

When I had my second-born, I had no idea her strong and beautiful spirit would grow and she would become one of my best and most understanding friends as an adult. It wasn't always like this. The day she looked me directly in the eyes as an adolescent and told me no was the day I knew something had to change. She was refusing to take yet another spelling test or even study the words. This rebellion didn't happen out of the blue and it didn't develop overnight. It was a gradual breakdown in our communication as teacher to student and soon as mother to daughter. I had explored every imaginable diagnosis, learning style, and approach to homeschooling. I would have tried anything—except, *not* homeschooling her.

The breakdown in our homeschool journey was seeping into our everyday lives. I was allowing our struggles in the classroom to break down our mother-daughter relationship, and it was *not* okay.

If you've never known homeschooling or parenting desperation, it looks like tear-stained pleading with the Lord for answers. And sometimes those answers do not look like we expected or imagined. So, I hired a tutor for my daughter—a friend who had homeschooled her own children and was now an empty nester. This continued with great success for two years. My daughter proved to be an amazing learner and smart as a whip, and she did all her schoolwork daily. She learned to listen to others and learned well with a different authority figure other than me. Not one problem. Today, this daughter is one of my best friends and my business partner. We even parent and homeschool side by side—she with her five littles, and me with her four youngest siblings. Parenting and homeschooling—together.

Don't ever sacrifice your relationships for the sake of homeschooling. It isn't worth it.

## HOMESCHOOLING IS A RELATIONSHIP

Living in deep and sincere relationships with others is hard work. To give the best and get the most out of your homeschooling, view your role as not only an educator, but the following roles associated with this relationship.

Homeschooling moms will feel pulled in many directions. They will have many names, and many shoes to fill, but only one name carries the most weight: *Mother.*

Nurturer, communicator, encourager, corrector, cheerleader, manager—just a few names of the roles we will cover later and that we carry as mothers but that also crossover into our homeschooling days as teachers. While we are always "mom," even in the schoolroom, the truth is some areas of our own character come out differently as mothers as the seasons of our homeschooling change.

Please don't read this as: take off your motherhood hat and put on a homeschooling hat. We don't leave our motherhood in the bedroom when we show up to the classroom. Our children are still called to a loving and expected standard of respect and be-havior toward us as their parent while we are homeschooling.

Lean in close as I share a tidbit of what I have learned in thirty-two years of parenting and twenty-six years of homeschooling: Just as our hours investing in teaching our children will match the hefty heart investment we give them to help them grow, our hours can never be counted simply as "just homeschooling." What you are doing is so much more. Your days will leave a trail of invest-ment in your home and into their future, and there is no way to curate a perfect day for such holy and heavy work.

In today's culture, we see carefully designed social media images filled with clean and decorated homeschool rooms, littles and teens quietly sitting at tables, explorations in the great outdoors, and end-less stacks of literature and smiling faces in every picture. These images do not portray resistance, lack of motivation, a trail of un-done chores, laziness or conflict, the sometimes herculean effort of growing our kids in character and love for one another, or the aftermath of hours of homeschooling and mothering well. There is no way to perfectly create an image of the investment you are making daily. Your home may not reflect any semblance of accom-plishment at the end of the day, but the fruit doesn't fit into a daily snapshot. It is in the panoramic view.

## OUR OTHER ROLES

There is a difference in how we parent and how we teach. We want to think there is a clean line of distinction and we can show up and be both. Don't be afraid of being both, and don't shy away from drawing the line and being "just mother," or "just teacher." This is vital to the health of your homeschool and your children knowing just "who" is showing up.

You will always be "mom" first. As a homeschool mom, many of your roles will stay the same. In any role we must step into during a given day, be careful not to sacrifice your relationships at the cost of being the teacher, the manager, or the corrector. We may struggle to find a balance in being mom and being the homeschool mom who needs to enforce and communicate that the schoolwork must get done. Be gentle in your approach, use discernment when you need to change your roles, and remember, you are always their mom. Remind them of this daily.

*Manager*

This is your biggest area for potential growth, and all your other names and roles fall under this one. You are the manager of your home and school. It is not a title we often like or feel we are doing well. We didn't take a course on home and school management, and some days, we really don't feel like showing up to this work. The crossover of managing home and school is one role and your whole schedule, approach, fine-tuned processes, and even the tone of your voice will relay this every day as you manage it all.

Don't be afraid of this role. Your management skills will grow, and your children will learn to listen to your management voice and respond accordingly. This will always be a part of who you are if you are mom and teacher. You cannot separate this role or name from your homeschooling, otherwise you will be a ship without a sail. Work on recognizing how your management ability, or lack of, affects your homeschooling and focus on areas you can improve.

## Nurturer

Each of your children will see homeschooling differently. They may adapt, embrace, or resist showing up on any given day. As mother, you can approach their unique thoughts and feelings about this transition and yearly decision with sensitivity. You can ask questions, engage in conversations, address fears, or celebrate the excitement.

As teacher, you will need to engage in ways to meet them where they are when it is time to do the work, and you will need to listen and look for the ways in which they uniquely learn. You may not know what sparks their minds, tugs on their imaginations, or builds confidence and motivation.

## Communicator

How we speak is just as important as what we say. When we are in mom mode, our tone and expectations might be more hurried, patient, or to the point. We may give our children ample time to listen and adapt, or we may explain and reexplain a task. We cohabitate with our children 24/7, and our communication isn't always the sweetest. As their teacher, we can carry over our maternal voices, but the communication level is one of the biggest areas of shifting we need to consider when we evaluate our relationships, effective learning, and the uniqueness of our children. Learning to listen and recognize what is being retained are the best tools we can bring to our teaching.

Each of your children has learned your intentions by the different tones in your voice as mom. They have been trained to listen, to react, to obey, or even to wait until your tone indicates urgency, impatience, seriousness, comfort, tenderness, or conversation. They know when you mean what you say and say what you mean, and they have pretty much figured you out as mom. Believe it or not, you have a tone for everything. Your children may not recognize or respond to your tones as teacher as you instruct, correct, and explain to their eager or struggling ears.

*Encourager*

An encourager is part of being both a mom and teacher. Some of us are natural encouragers; and some struggle to know what to say and when. Each of our children receive encouragement uniquely, and so, learning about our children comes first. Study their words, motivation, and emotional needs to know how you can best encourage them. Focus on the areas in which they need to be encouraged and the areas where they are already confident.

As a mom to many children, I learned quickly which children thrived from words of encouragement in matters of the heart and home—which usually applied to their schoolwork as well. Even before an assignment began, some of my children were motivated by my encouragement and my acknowledgment of their abilities. Because of that, they finished strong. Some of my children needed continual affirmation during the process, and others just looked forward to the prize of accomplishment and nothing more.

Encouragement didn't always equate to words. Sometimes my presence, or my releasing them in trust to finish their work independently spoke volumes enough. Remember, your tone matters and that encouragement from a teacher is recognizing the specifics of the struggle, achievement, or focused work and not just encouragement as a child or person. Give them motivation in increments and encouragement via academic help and not just through motivational speech. Homeschooling encouragement often equates to hands-on help or repetitive work. I encourage you to study your child and learn how they receive encouragement and what motivates them. You will begin to learn just as much about yourself as you do your child in this process.

Perhaps encouragement doesn't come naturally to you or maybe your words are 95 percent instruction and 5 percent encouragement. Because you love your child and want the best for them, this role as encourager will grow on you, and them, as you begin to see the fruit of this effort.

## Corrector

This role may make us cringe, whether mother or teacher—at least it does for me. I know I must, and I do, correct my children in everyday life to raise them as humble, respectful, and responsible people. But, when I show up to the schoolroom, I would love to just read our favorite books with soft music playing in the background; map out our geography; assign a few math problems; and wrap up with our writing and a science unit study and call it a day.

This is not reality on most days. There will be red correction marks on math problems, eraser marks on sloppy and careless work, and a tone of correction to regain an environment condu-cive to learning amid the wiggles and giggles and interruptions. (Because, hey, they are kids, and they won't do the right thing every day. Neither will we.) This name causes the most discour-agement for the mom as teacher. You may feel like you are always in corrector mode, and this is all your kids know you as. You just want to be their mom. Our kids get weary of correction from one person all day long, so this is the name you will need to season with words of grace as you depend on the Lord's wisdom and back up at the end of the day when you feel like all you have done is "be the corrector."

### Cheerleader

If we could be cheerleaders all day every day and nothing else, I don't think we'd hear any complaints from our families. Some-times, we can get super creative, energetic, and even highly in-vested into rolling quite a few of the names we carry all into one cheerleading outfit. Some days, we show up and realize that today is a day everyone in our homeschool needs a little cheering up and every other name doesn't really matter in those moments. I call this grace and space for what is needed and when.

I don't want to throw a wet towel on the party, but a word of caution to the overly zealous cheerleaders who shy away from be-ing the correctors: you'll miss the most foundational parts of your squad formation and may need to reevaluate your reasons for how you show up to homeschool. We can become blind to the messi-ness, mistakes, and lackadaisical efforts and behavior of our chil-dren so that we primarily show up as the cheerleader. Positivity minus correction can produce pride in our children, and their motivation for success may be expectant on your praise, minus edification.

Cheering our kids on in their academics primarily looks like motivational goals, reinforcing the work they are doing, celebrating the wins and acknowledging the losses, giving tips and help when needed, showing up when they grow discouraged, acknowledging effort over success, and calling them up to a standard of celebration they did not know they could achieve. You will always be their biggest cheerleader, so don't feel bad when you also must be the corrector.

## PARENT OR TEACHER

We know the many benefits of homeschooling include more time and space to foster, grow, and invest in stronger relationships with our children. Spending more time together at home can be a blessing and a challenge.

While we will learn more about our children's interests, strengths, and weaknesses, most of our homeschooling will focus on academics, activities, and enrichment. When we are picking out curriculums, considering our children's learning styles, setting up our school spaces, and mapping out our year, we rarely plan how we will approach our relationships. Finding balance is tricky because you are in parenting mode until it is time to become "teacher."

Does the parenting stop? No. But how do you navigate this delicate balance well? There is so much to balance: expectations, time management, neatness, corrections, listening, completing the work, as well as fostering those good habits of communication. We should, and always will, be the parent first. Truthfully, some days, we want to be "just mom" or "just dad."

When all the schoolwork is done, we may feel too tired to show up and be the fun, engaged, and present parent. We become too stretched and have given so much of ourselves to be an amazing *homeschool* parent that we save very little for our other parenting moments. Remember, your relationships with your children are more vital than homeschooling. Begin there.

······· *personal reflection* ·······

Is it my greatest joy to be my child's parent and teacher?

······· *personal challenge* ·······

No one knows and loves my child more than I do. I will not hold too tightly to a badge of personal expectations or a vision of success that could cost me a relationship with my child. I will remember that God called me to motherhood, parenting, and loving my child before I was called to homeschool.

······· *drawing from the well* ·······

God has a plan in motion for our children, and our time with them while homeschooling feels so vast yet is part of a small piece of His perfect power that will carry on for generations to come.

*"Now to him who is able to do far more abundantly than all that we ask or think, according to the power at work within us, to him be glory in the church and in Christ Jesus throughout all generations, forever and ever. Amen."* Ephesians 3:20–21

···· *a prayer for my homeschool* ····

Lord, today I fall before Your throne in humble adoration. I need Your strength and wisdom to show up for my family and to be all the names they need me to be. Help me to receive Your peace, and show my family grace, as together we live out this calling in our home and school. May *Your* name be on our lips today. You are the giver of all good gifts. Thank You for allowing me to be mom and teacher in this season. In Jesus' name, Amen.

# chapter 4

# Frustrations, Fears, and Feeling Fed Up

*I* used to be the "yelling mom" and the "uptight homeschooling mom." These titles never defined me before I became a mother or before I began homeschooling; but then, I'd never had to schedule my life around other people, and I'd never felt so responsible for the well-being and lifelong learning of a human being before. Motherhood is hard, rewarding work, and then we add education and enrichment to our list of responsibilities daily and our overwhelm comes out in the areas yet to be "refined."

I say this with all humility as a mama who has been and continues to be refined and shaped into a better mother, a better person. Behind our own homeschooling doors and schedules, we experience the real-life, frustrating, and escalating moments that can lead us to raise our voices . . . and our eruptions, which never defined us, at least until we started homeschooling. Remember, you may be feeling pressed down, shaken, and tangled, trying to make sure everyone not only gets a little piece of you daily, but also the best of you.

And then you "lose it." Later, in disbelief and angry retrospection, we wonder how we keep losing our cool.

I began to track the patterns of my days to identify triggers to my reactions and responses. I noticed verbal cues I would say calmly on repeat before my frustration got the best of all of us. One day, I sat with my children around the school table doing a group unit study and waiting (not so patiently) for the hundredth time that day for one of them to finish using the bathroom. All learning was on hold while sounds of water splashing in the sink and carefree humming grated on my nerves, and I heard my voice raise a decibel as I called to that child that we were done waiting. This was the day my frustrations began to form a pattern my children began to tiptoe around and learn to navigate in our homeschool days.

Was my behavior godly and good? No. Did I want to have better control and be the relaxed homeschool mama with the calm demeanor? Yes. Little things grew into bigger things because I hadn't made space for myself to breathe or reset. I hadn't realized my own emotional boundaries or recognized the signs that I was reaching my emotional capacity. I hadn't set boundaries for our homeschool spaces. My frustrations were getting the best of me; I needed Jesus, and a change of heart and perspective, and some space. We all need space when we homeschool!

The longer I homeschooled, the less frustrated I would become during moments like these. I became frustrated by a long laundry list I kept mentally adding to every time we didn't finish our work for the day; every time the house looked like a tornado had swept through and everyone else now had free time; every time I had to repeat an instruction or raise my voice to enforce my expectations.

## GIVE YOURSELF SPACE AND GRACE

A list of *what* frustrates us can actually be used to help us identify and legitimize *where* these feelings are coming from. We can then be ready to meet those moments with solutions. Often, we are unaware of the small unspoken frustrations we have. Until I began noticing the words or thoughts I would mutter under my breath or share with my husband, I had no idea these thought patterns had been growing a frustration in me to the point of being fed up. Although they were small "innocent" thoughts, words, or comparisons to traditional schools, I was a silent storm waiting to happen.

Below are a few common thoughts homeschooling moms feel and express. Read through these frustrations and add some of your own. This is a safe place to identify *where* or *why* you are feeling fed up.

- I am with my kids all day, so I rarely get time to myself for a break.
- Daycare for my youngest children isn't an option for us financially. I am not able to give my little ones enough attention while I am teaching.
- Since my kids don't attend a traditional school, lunches aren't prepared by cafeteria staff.
- There are no substitute teachers to step in when I have an appointment.
- There's no janitor to clean up the house at night.
- There's no principal to handle disruptions.
- Our greatest moments of triumph are rarely witnessed or celebrated by anybody. The day goes on, and then it's time

to make dinner or drive to an extracurricular activity.

- Sometimes I feel like my non-homeschooling friends and relatives are waiting for us to fail.

The first step to starting strong is to not give up. Giving up is a series of moments of being fed up. So, what shifted and changed for me? I gave myself space and grace. This isn't a cliché. I began to find small spaces in my day that were "mine." I would get my kiddos settled with daily quiet time activities, chores, rest time, or reading, and I would step away to go for a walk, exercise, shower, or make a new list when I realized functioning by the current list that day would prove futile and frustrating. I would write a note that read, "Knock only in an emergency," and stick it on my door at my kids' eye level. As my children grew older, I would find a daily time to step away from the house, away from them, away from anything that remotely called my name to do something.

Not being able to get away for a time is quite possible. That was my situation for many years. But learning how to make the space where and when you can *is* the most necessary step, even if this means you are home with your kiddos and your space is a sacred time of non-interruption. It doesn't have to be a social media worthy space of rest or a coffee shop retreat. It can be earbuds, your favorite podcast, or Bible reading. It can be a hot bath.

When life is finally quiet and we are settled in those spaces, it is critical to give yourself grace, just as the Lord extends grace to us. A gentle word of caution when you finally have some time to think: don't be too hard on yourself and overthink all the other things you could be doing with this space.

By giving yourself grace and space, you can avoid meltdowns, both for you and your children. Here are some ways that help.

- Stick to what is essential in a day and avoid overcommitting.
- Include fun activities in the day. Take your schoolwork to the park. Pack a picnic. Make it a museum day. Homeschool with friends for a day.
- Take more breaks. Try a mid-morning break. Change your school schedule to four days a week. Get everyone moving and break for the sunshine and laughter.
- Invest in self-care: take a daily walk, find time for a nap, meet with a friend.
- Each day, have everyone do one thing that blesses another person in the family. Complete someone's chore for them, write a note of encouragement, or make a special treat.
- Pivot in moments of stress. Change the plan or the mood of the day.
- Prepare ahead for the predictable homeschooling triggers.
- Make a list of alternative responses for those moments.
- Have a family meeting and create solutions.
- Get help. Find a good counselor, a regular babysitter, a tutor for the high schoolers, a co-op of friends.
- Find the root of your most fed-up moments and work on those outside of homeschooling.
- Study your children. Know how they think; anticipate how they will act or may react to certain subjects and unexpected changes. Many times, we can see a conflict before it happens.

More noteworthy, every day we need to make a sacred space for Jesus. The time to lay our burdens at His feet and to ask Him to help us be prepared for the day ahead. He doesn't call us to suffer alone. He calls us to persevere, but also gives us wisdom. He will give you wisdom, discernment, and grace for every day. His Word reminds us that "the steadfast love of the LORD never ceases; his mercies never come to an end; they are new every morning; great is your faithfulness" (Lam. 3:22–23).

The more we draw near to Jesus, the more we will recognize our need for time with Him every day. Frustrations are our reaction to situations, but there is a subtle and sneaky word called fear that can motivate us to make decisions and dictate responses in our homeschooling. Our homeschooling fears are not easily identifiable because fear is not an action that is in our face daily. It lies beneath the surface, and it takes insight and evaluation to make sure our reactions are not motivated by fear.

## WHAT AM I AFRAID OF?

I am not going to sugarcoat fear. In fact, fear can be both good and bad. Fear can be healthy, if we allow it to have the right place and the right power in our lives. Yet, fear can also cripple us, hold us back, and squash the confidence that initially helped us make the decision to homeschool. Homeschooling sets us apart. Homeschooling gives the world a front row seat to a different way of raising and educating children that some consider a foolish experiment. Even when we don't have naysayers speaking words of doubt directly into our ears, we know the world is watching and waiting. Fear makes us hide. Fear makes us quiet, and fear seeps into the cracks of all our decisions. Even the decision to home-school. Especially homeschooling.

I began homeschooling in the dark ages. I was in the minority, while a handful of homeschooling families were also "trying it out." There were many voices, spoken and unspoken. There were doubts and uncertainty. Collectively, we all had more questions than an-swers and took each step with a great deal of fear. We forged on with a small community, few curriculum choices, sharing our limited experiences with one another. Homeschooling today is a dichot-omy of anxiety caused by information overload and the valuable resources now available to us to calm our fears. That is the sneaky thing about fear. It comes from too little or too much information and because we are worried that we aren't going to get it right in the end. Fear affects our decisions and our relationships. It holds us back from progress and the fullness of His promises.

Read through the most common fears homeschooling parents will face. Often, decisions are made from fear, but knowing where our fears lie is the first step to name them and surrender them. Fear has no place in your homeschooling.

I am inadequate.
My mistakes will harm my children.
I am worried I will leave too many gaps.
I may receive criticism.
I fear not getting the support I need.
I'm afraid we won't finish well.
My relationships with my children will suffer.
My kids will miss opportunities.

I am afraid I will lose motivation.

What if I lose my patience?

I won't be able to manage it all.

The list could go on. But rather than make a long list of fears, let's identify solutions and ways to combat them. Fear in homeschooling can be exhaustive and exhausting, but knowing truth is the most powerful weapon against fear, and this the Lord has given us in abundance.

When my three oldest transferred to a private school for their final years of high school, I was fearful of so many things. I was facing significant health challenges and had multiple grades and ages I was homeschooling. Sending them to a traditional high school was one of the hardest decisions I'd made, but a solution I so needed in this season of our homeschool journey. The day the terrific trio drove out of the driveway on the way to their first day of "real school," I was silently crying behind closed doors, gathering my wits to show up and teach my other kids.

But my fears never materialized. Our three oldest experienced the traditional school model for only a few years, and they adapted well: They ran for student council president and vice president and won. They created a worship team and led as a trio. They held (more than I can count) social gatherings and aced their tests. They were inducted into the National Honor Society, played sports, received scholarships, graduated with honors, and were loved.

*Homeschooling in fear casts doubt on our children
and our own abilities.*

My kids reminded me again that fear is a liar. My kids lived the truth and the confidence that a homeschooler can thrive when presented with new opportunities, while pursuing excellence.

## FACING OUR FEARS

I am always reminded of the story of Esther when I know I need to put my faith before my fears. God had chosen Esther to take a path that required great obedience. Her life is an example of humility and obedience to the difficult things, even when the cost is great. God equipped Queen Esther to go before King Ahasuerus. Her courage and strength were fortified by faithful steps of obedience. Faith can overcome our fears. God doesn't leave us alone in our callings. He is in every detail, and we can trust Him to meet us on the path He has called us to.

Fear could have stopped Esther at any moment. She faced the king when she was afraid. God went before her.

Fear could have silenced her when she worried about the outcome. She spoke in confidence and was not controlled by fear.

Fear could have changed the trajectory of the lives of her people. She made a plan and put her fear aside.

Esther had no control in any outcome she was presented with. When we relinquish control, we allow our faith to overcome fear.

If you know that homeschooling is what God is asking of you, then it's time to let your faith overcome your fears. Ask God to equip you with everything you need. Taking the step of obedience is the first step to trusting him.

The antidote to fear is acknowledging we are not in control. Below are good reminders to keep before you every day. Your homeschooling future doesn't need to be cut short because your frustrations and fears got in the way. Read them out loud and say your name either before each sentence or at the end. Speak life into your homeschooling daily. May these strong reminders of truth help squash your doubts and fears.

- Silence the voices of doubt.
- Ignore the naysayers.
- Find your tribe.
- Set high expectations and allow room for grace.
- Just begin.
- Acknowledge you will make mistakes.
- Prepare and plan not to fail.

## ······· *personal reflection* ·······

What have I taken on and feel overwhelmed with that someone else can do? In which areas do I feel I have lost control? Where do I need grace and strength from the Lord? Am I the "yelling mom"? If so, when am I most triggered to raise my voice, or when do I feel the most stress?

## ······· *personal challenge* ·······

When I find myself in a holding pattern of stress, reaction, remorse, conviction, or desperation, I will find a quiet space to clear my mind, pray, rest, and ask God for His grace. I will give myself the priority of space and grace today.

## ······· *drawing from the well* ·······

God calls us to an abundant life, where fear does not hold us back and His mercies are new every morning. Ask Him to be your portion today. Do not lean on your own understanding. His mercies never fail.

> *"My flesh and my heart may fail,*
> *but God is the strength of my heart and my portion forever."*
> Psalm 73:26

## ···· *a prayer for my homeschool* ····

Lord, I give You the glory for all You have done in and through my children's lives and learning. I turn control back over to You, so my children will see an example of surrender and balanced servant leadership. In Jesus' name, Amen.

*chapter 5*

· · · · · · · · · · · · · ·

# Pursuing Excellence

*It* will be easy to get distracted from your first job as a home-school mom: to teach your children. There will be a lot of choices you have to make each day as you navigate how you spend your time, and the more comfortable you become in your teaching, the more opportunities you will want to try. One of the foremost questions any homeschool mom needs to answer is, "What is best for my child?"

Many shiny things can come along and pull our attention away or avert our gaze from our priority. We may think we are doing our very best by signing up for ministry opportunities, service projects, hands-on outdoor activities, and all the choices for curriculum we want to change out every year. But despite the value of these things, they can actually be distractions, and distractions are deceiving. We must learn to discern between the wisest choice and every choice that turns the head. Some things we can't control, but most distractions pull our eyes, hands, and thoughts away from our priority to invest in our children in the short time we have each day.

Distractions come in many forms. You may find choosing your homeschooling style takes you in many directions, and sometimes navigating this is distracting to our primary focus of teaching. I discovered that choosing the easiest options for my personal schedule wasn't always the best fit for my children. What may seem a more relaxed approach could be robbing our children of structure and the lesson of perseverance. What may feel like a sabbatical for us could be the very thing that propels us away from routine and accomplishing the work that needs to be done.

Let's be careful to avoid "filling our homeschool" with convenience and activity or performance for the sake of calling it a day.

Distracted homeschooling can add up to a lot of shiny activities and free time, but that is just a model of a distracted life.

Distracted homeschooling convinces us that "at least" our children are not in public school and that "anything" is better than that.

Distracted homeschooling makes us feel like we are doing our best when in truth our kids are just getting the leftovers.

Read through the most common symptoms of distraction in your homeschooling below. Put a checkmark by those that stand out to you as something you are experiencing and may need to change.

### The Distracted Homeschooler

☐ My child's reading and arithmetic are at the bottom of the priority list.
☐ My child exhibits trouble with attention span and consistent listening.
☐ My child struggles with academics due to inconsistency.

☐ My child struggles with respect and diligence.

☐ Our time away from home trumps time at home.

☐ Our outside commitments exceed our time for school.

☐ Our social opportunities have become more frequent.

☐ I change curriculum even when the current plan is working well.

☐ Self-learning and independent work trump parent-led homeschooling, grading, and evaluations.

## The Focused Homeschooler

☐ Creates a plan and follows with perseverance

☐ Allows for flexibility, but still gets the work done

☐ Recognizes areas that need work

☐ Finds the curriculum for each child that works best for them and sticks to it

☐ Balances time between parent-led teaching and raising independent learners

☐ Realizes being the "teacher" and staying home to get the work done are priorities

☐ Uses free time and social activities as part of homeschooling and not the sole education

☐ Finds and makes time to grow and work on character and matters of the heart in their homeschooling

☐ Works their schedule around homeschooling vs. homeschooling around a schedule

☐ Children can focus when listening and can demonstrate an eagerness to learn

Homeschooling my children from my bedroom wasn't a choice I made. Sickness never asks permission to enter your life and it certainly does not respect time or family, let alone homeschooling multiple children. When my husband, Dan, had to return to work after I delivered our babies, we "got through." When my children were down with a cold, flu, or something more serious, we would homeschool from the couch, with a feverish child in my arms. Books, papers, and children were scattered around me as we worked through their lessons, and reading time was a comfort and not a "to-do." This all worked out okay.

I learned to pivot and so did my kids. I cannot promise you by the end of the day, when my husband would walk through the door, I would be all smiles and the homeschooling setting before his eyes was social media worthy. I would often fall into bed exhausted and worried those evenings when life would take over my homeschooling and I wondered if we really pursued excellence in the learning moments we had that day. Sometimes, it wasn't newborns, or sickness, or even an unforeseen circumstance, but a level of knowing some days we show up and absolutely cannot sustain a high-level output and choose to focus on the very best and leave the rest. This isn't a cop-out, an opt-out, or even a way out but rather a shift in mindset.

*Knowing your homeschool and tracking progress and priorities allows you the flexibility to choose on days when life chooses for you.*

Life chose sickness and rest for me when I had multiple grades and ages to homeschool, and I had to attend to my health. I cried many tears to my husband that this would be a forever memory for my children, and I didn't want this to be the version of homeschooling they would remember. For over one year of this specific season, a typical day would consist of my older kiddos initiating the household morning routines, and in new, systematic rotation they would show up at my bedroom door with their crate of schoolbooks and readers and climb up next to me to "do school." So many questions about what homeschooling with excellence looked like clouded my vision in moments like this. I knew I was showing up the best I could. I knew I wasn't giving up when I could keep going. I knew my children were learning on a consistent and regular basis. So, why did this season of our homeschooling feel not so excellent? I had forgotten that my children were learning well and living well, and I had made an idol out of something conjured up in a list of expectations and comparison born of worry. A daily surrender to the Ultimate Planner and Perfecter of my faith and my daily life was the only way I could truly homeschool well in this season of unknowns.

During this year, I embraced excellence in our homeschooling in all new ways. My children didn't need to change, their curriculum was still perfect for them individually, our family unit was still strong, and homeschooling continued to be a priority for us.

I learned a lot about myself and where my expectations in our homeschooling journey had taken me.

I learned the areas I had falsely allowed to fill a mental and emotional checklist of excellence in homeschooling, when perhaps they had become fillers or placeholders—areas to replace true excellence that required more of me showing up and fewer activities or fluff learning to say we did school.

I learned that excellence is an attitude, a mindset, an approach to what you can do and realizing what you cannot do.

I learned I expected more of myself than I could give, and I required more of my kids in unnecessary areas.

*Choosing the best and leaving the rest gives a homeschooling mom the tools to homeschool with priority and pursue excellence.*

When my kiddos scrambled onto my queen bed with their schoolwork, our space was limited, the distractions could have been overwhelming, and the complaints could have piled up. What I thought would grow to be my children's worst formative memories of our homeschooling seasons ended up being the best, most adventurous, focused learning we ever had.

My children received one-on-one learning times with me. I couldn't leave the room, take a call or visitor, or schedule an activity.

My children learned to read to an audience of many as we gathered and fit in more books, stories, and discussions together. We took an entire literary journey together that year.

My children loved being in my space and purposed to make it a place of comfort. This was in turn a blessing to us all. Our school space became a place of healing for us all.

My children learned more compassion and independence. They showed up when I felt like I could not, and we met our daily lesson goals together. My children learned the essential things in their academics and life, and the rest we left for another day, month, year.

We became a team of professional schedulers, meal-makers, dishwashers, potty-trainers, readers, letter writers, laundry washers, poetry reciters, spelling and math fact masters, and real-life homeschoolers pursuing excellence.

We did the thing that mattered the most. We showed up and gave it our all.

## HOW TO HOMESCHOOL WITH EXCELLENCE

Choosing the best for our children will often mean we have to set aside many things that are distracting us. Not until I took the time to assess where we were spending our time and to evaluate my children's progress did I notice patterns of distractions or lack of focus.

The following questions are a good starting point for your own pursuit of excellence in your homeschool:

- Recognize and identify areas you are distracted easily.
- Identify areas within your home that pull you away from the most necessary things.
- Set personal goals for yourself and your children per quarter.
- Limit the extra activities or distractions in your homeschool if you are not completing the academics.
- Consider the areas where you have filled in your time to take the easier route or in the name of unschooling.
- Keep records of your reading per family member and discuss the material.
- Keep track of your children's progress in a way you can identify growth beyond your observations.
- Track the time you have committed to focused homeschooling time with your family.
- Evaluate your personal expectations with a realistic level of achievement.

*personal reflection*

Have I become distracted with my choices in homeschooling? Am I spending more time focused on other pursuits than I am teaching my children? Where can I regain some balance in both homeschooling and enrichment activities for us all, but not ignore the importance of one over the other?

*personal challenge*

I will remember that my circumstances do not have to be perfect to homeschool well. Today, I surrender my expectations and will draw from the well of knowledge and discernment the Lord will give to me when I seek Him. I commit to pursuing excellence in all that I do to bring God the glory in our homeschool.

*drawing from the well*

There will always be exceptions to our seasons, our family dynamics, our children's learning styles, and our time. Let's ask ourselves, "Am I pursuing excellence?"

*"Not that we are sufficient in ourselves to claim anything as coming from us, but our sufficiency is from God, who has made us sufficient to be ministers of a new covenant, not of the letter but of the Spirit. For the letter kills, but the Spirit gives life."* 2 Corinthians 3:5–6

*a prayer for my homeschool*

Lord, I come to You as a homeschool mama who needs Your strength and perseverance in my everyday. Help me to lead my children in Your way and in the areas You have gifted them, for Your glory and honor. Give me wisdom and the discernment to teach my children Your precepts and teach them well in their studies. In Jesus' name, Amen.

*chapter 6*

- - • • • • • • • • • • • • • •

# Multiple Children, Grades, and Ages

*P*erhaps you scrolled through the table of contents and this chapter caught your eye because this is your life. The feelings of urgency and overwhelm while managing multiple grades and ages can feel insurmountable. Often our feelings dictate our homeschooling. Maybe your home feels like crazy town, and all you would like is a bit of sanity. Many days you are left wondering if you are doing enough and how you will be able to sustain this level of commitment and expectations.

While homeschooling our ten children over a span of three decades, there'd be days I'd wake up creating a mental plan for the day before I even got out of bed. I couldn't find enough hours in the day to homeschool them each adequately, and I was spreading myself too thin trying to make it all happen. I didn't want my older children to grow up with a strong dislike for homeschooling, feeling as if they had been denied a good education or were just convenient babysitters of their younger siblings.

These were legitimate concerns that invaded my mind when I went to bed each night. The reality was that there were a lot of children and only one of me, but I took our homeschooling seriously enough to find a solution. After several rough seasons of juggling multiple ages and grade levels as well the responsibilities of our home and personal life, I was thankful to find myself in a rhythm of homeschooling and finding peace and calm in the mix. That didn't mean the plan was void of hard work, but after creating a plan and working out the bugs, I realized this can be done!

As we care for babies and toddlers and homeschool kids ages four to seventeen, we are also planning, preparing, and overseeing meals, playtime, naps, nursing, spelling tests, reading, music lessons, and doing our best to keep our head above water. This much output could easily consume our day. We are trying to configure a normal homeschool plan and stretch our attention in many different directions. The strain may cause us to ask ourselves:

Am I failing my children by choosing to homeschool so many children at once?

Will my kids only remember the bad days?

Will homeschooling become an unpleasant memory for them?

Before we go any further, let's do the Homeschooling Report Card exercise together. This especially applies to parents schooling multiple ages and grades. I do this every year before I begin or after we have started, and I am facing new giants that need some troubleshooting. Don't let the words "report card" intimidate you. Before any solution or fix can be found, you have to get to the root of the problem areas. This will help you identify the areas where you are doing well and the areas where you need the most support.

*Homeschooling Report Card*

*True or False:*

1. Homeschooling will look the same whether I am teaching one student or ten.
2. I am doing well with multitasking my home responsibilities and caring for many people, but when it comes to academics, I need help.
3. I am doing well with the core subjects, but I need a *lot* of help caring for my little ones during school hours.
4. I am managing the academics well, but I need more help with managing my home because I spend most of my day teaching.
5. It is cost prohibitive for me to homeschool so many grades and ages. I need ideas!
6. I do not feel equipped with the right resources to do this.
7. I am doing well with the resources but could use some ideas in the scheduling area.
8. I feel like I am failing my kids.
9. My expectations are balanced; I am struggling to achieve the result.
10. I believe we can do this.

While there's no scoring or "grade" associated with this exercise, your report card will give you a starting point for assessing your strengths and the areas to work on. Note that I did not say "weaknesses." I like to view our homeschooling as a path of learning and growing with our kids.

Your answers to the report card questions will help you gauge where you need to begin managing realistic expectations for your homeschool experience. Recognizing the individual needs of each child as you consider your overall homeschool plan will help you define expectations in all areas. This is a helpful step to starting your homeschool with fresh eyes every year. When I took the time to evaluate all of our needs collectively, I was able to manage my expectations with a more realistic approach. It is easy to make an elaborate homeschool plan, but the true success is where we meet the needs of our children individually.

## MANAGING YOUR EXPECTATIONS

If you are struggling to know what to expect from homeschooling, consider your children individually and then collectively. I took an afternoon and a notebook page or two for each of my children separately. I was amazed to see it all written out on paper. Write out the expectations you have for each child for their academics. Your list will help them set goals to meet appropriate academic requirements and standards. Next, write out a list of achievable goals for your child in areas of personal growth. You can use this list to help your child track their progress throughout the year.

Then, ask yourself the following questions to help you move forward:

1. Am I expecting too much from my children and myself?
2. Are my expectations realistic and goal driven?
3. Have I evaluated the needs and the goals of my children individually?

4. Are my expectations manageable and sustainable?

Once you have spent time reevaluating expectations, you will break these into areas of growth for each of your children individually and as a group. I've included a sample notebook page in this section to show how I lay this out each year for each of my children. Using a loose notebook or any special homeschool planner of your choice, create a plan per child that lists core academic subjects, as well as chores, character growth, service or ministry opportunities, spiritual formation, peer time and friendships, values, and new skills.

This is one of my favorite things to do because I have each of my children's strengths, academic needs, short-term, and even long-term goals laid out in front of me as I plan their homeschooling year. Skipping this step increases the likelihood that you will live in fear of neglecting to teach necessary skills and lessons. And fear reigns over confidence and peace.

You know your child best, and considering the whole child will give you peace because there's a long-term vision rather than a fear-based scramble every day.

Below is a list of areas to consider as you begin your process of homeschooling your children as individuals and not as a collective group. Yes, practically speaking, homeschooling multiple grades and ages will require some group learning, and this element can be a wonderful tool to help with scheduling. You will consider the following areas in relation to each child as you map out their plan for the school year. Enjoy this process. It will truly bless you as their mom. You will discover their areas of interest you may not have tapped into yet. Their weaknesses and strengths, gifts and needs will flow onto the paper and give insight and sensitivity as you plan their homeschool journey.

This example note page is filled in with examples of ideas for creating your own page for each of your children. In each category, fill in your own goals and ideas for each child. This exercise in vision planning and evaluation will help you consider their individual needs before you create your homeschool plan as a family.

---

[Child's Name]  [Academic Year]  [Age]

Academic Goals

Math: Master multiplication tables; foster critical thinking
Handwriting: Neater penmanship; letter writing; formatting
Reading: One book a week; book reports with improved penmanship and formatting; move up one reading level; improved comprehension
Spelling: Complete new spelling book; master all phonics blends and faster speed drills

---

Character Goals

Self-control and more emotional awareness
Responsibility and diligence in schoolwork and chores
Kindness to others outside the home
Perseverance when things are hard; not giving up
Listening when spoken to and answering the first time

---

Social

More confidence in making friends
More peer group get-togethers
Learn discernment and how to identify good friendships
Play dates once a week
Begin new sport and church activities

---

Interests

Volunteer at the local animal shelter to foster love and care for animals

Take a watercolor class to foster artistic abilities

Visit the Science Center and hands-on labs and classes to pursue science interests

Read a new book series

Set up workstation for experiments and hands-on building projects

Go on nature hikes with camera to develop and research the science fields of interest

Allow more time in the kitchen helping to grow curiosity in food preparation and new interest in baking

Responsibilities

Add/change new household chores to expand abilities

Make bed more regularly

Learn to do laundry and put away clothes

Minimize screen time

Physical Goals

Regular and daily exercise

Consistent bedtime on school nights

Improved self-care with less prompting or reminders

Assess appearance before leaving the house

Skin care routine

Spiritual Goals

More conversations about personal struggles

Begin personal devotional tracking and checklist

Relationship Goals

Getaway with one parent to have a deeper conversation about sex, relationships, and boundaries

Relationship Goals cont.

Foster stronger friendships
Find solutions for sibling rivalry; learn more patience and grace
More consistent youth group attendance

---

[Child's Name] Personal Feedback

What would you like to learn this year in addition to your school-
work?
What do you think would be a fun outlet to learn or try?
Do you like the friends you have, and why?
What areas of your chores and personal responsibility do you
think you do well already?
Are there things you find more difficult that frustrate you?
Is there one consistent activity you would like us to consider add-
ing to your schedule this year?

---

Recap: I see the potential of [name of child] growing in so many
areas this year. From academics to personal goals, I see an overarching need for confidence and responsibility. I think more
exposure to opportunities with other people and matching interests with more purposeful events, activities, and outlets will help
greatly.

---

## SCHEDULING THAT WORKS FOR YOU

You may not be a scheduling fan, but sometimes a back-pocket
schedule you can use on the days you don't want to just roll with
it will bring some order back to your day. With ten children and
homeschooling six under the age of nine in one season, I realized I would need more than just a few clever tips or scheduling
ideas. During the most intense homeschooling years, making a

schedule saved my sanity. I didn't use it to hold my children or myself captive but rather to clearly communicate daily expectations to each child. It is easy to get caught in the cycle of "circle" management, where you go around and around, and no child gets their work done because they are waiting for your direction and help. When everyone needs you to be the manager, what happens when you are overwhelmed, losing track of who did what, and can't keep up? Nothing gets done.

"Scheduling" sometimes can have a negative label attached. In a new culture of homeschooling where the trend is to take a more relaxed approach to our daily schedules and expectations, we have lost the value of order as a guide. By no means am I talking about a rigid and rigorous schedule that spoils the experience, but what happens to the plan you now have in mind for your child individually if you are continually just "rolling with it"?

Let's get into the nitty gritty as I share my secret recipe for homeschooling multiples well.

## GOING THROUGH THE MOTIONS: THE RULE OF FOUR

Consider yourself the hub of a wagon wheel. (Or any wheel for that matter.) You are basically the control center, keeping everyone and everything in balance as you homeschool multiple children daily. Every spoke attached to the hub continues to move in perfect sync with you as you manage everyone (all the spokes) all day. When and as you move, they move. Each spoke in your homeschool wheel will be propelled and guided by "the rule of four." I have used this as a guide to find calm and productivity when managing the homeschooling of many children.

The rule of four is explained in terms of our "motions." Each motion applies to all your children, and each involves the same time cycle. Think of this rule as a continuous circle of success. All four motions operate simultaneously for everyone involved, including you.

*Motion One: One-on-One Individual Learning with Mom*

This is your time with one of your children working on difficult subjects or lessons, listening to them read, or teaching them tricky penmanship, phonics, or math. You spend this time working with one or a few children near the same grade or learning level. Your teaching time will be spent on areas that need singular focus, and these children receive your undivided attention. This time, for example, might include giving a spelling test or working on handwriting dictation. Or it might look like one-on-one reading for your child who may struggle and needs your attention . . . or studying math concepts or corrections that are specific to a child's grade and needs.

You are not hovering over them and toggling your mind and body from room to room; your eyes aren't darting here and there to check on the status of everyone else in the house, the laundry, a phone call, or anything that might pull you away. This is focused time between you and your child. They know they have your attention, and you commit to the best of your best ability. Sometimes, this means you have a baby in your lap or in the highchair next to you with an activity to occupy them, but you are very present and stationary.

*Motion Two: Household Tasks, Chores, or Practice Times*

If your children do not have any home responsibilities, this might be part of your growing list of things "undone" in your home at the end of the homeschool day. Make a list of every little or big chore that can be done without you or with some initial teaching and modeling. Have a lesson day that consists of showing your children how to accomplish a household task or chore and assign these according to age or capability. Many little tasks undone can lead to an overwhelming sense that nothing is ever done.

Pair an older child with a younger child to ensure your time is kept open for teaching your other children. While they are busy cleaning their rooms, practicing piano, preparing snacks, or working with their buddy, you are spending that one-on-one time with the other children. This rotation continues throughout the day, ensuring all practice times, chores, and tasks are done by the end of the school day.

We cannot assume our children will know how to complete an assigned chore or task without a little guidance. Set aside some time to model and teach the task before expecting complete independence from your children during this motion. Every time a new chore was introduced in our home, I took a week to walk through the motions and expectations with them.

One year, when I was adding the bathroom cleanup to the list of chores, I made a family announcement to meet me in the bathroom, also adding that my children were to show up with their swimsuits on. Holding a scrub brush and wearing my swimsuit and rubber boots (for a successful, dramatic effect), I handed my phone to them, giving them permission to videotape me standing in the bathtub with the water running as I demonstrated how the bathroom was to be cleaned. Step by step, I made a fun video and entertaining experience for the purpose of modeling the expectations and for memory's sake. They, of course, never forgot this and had a clear visual of how to do this independently.

Once you teach, model, and assign tasks, you will not be needed for this motion. These tasks should not be time-consuming, and so music, sports, or individual practice times can fall into this motion.

*Motion Three: Group Learning*

Gather children of similar ages and choose subjects that can be taught at one "grade" level and in a group learning style. Consider subjects you can collaborate on that are topic based and not age specific. Some children will be working independently or doing their household chores at the same time you are using this group learning for similarly aged students. This could be a history timeline that focuses on memory work and historical facts and figures. Elementary science is also a wonderful group learning subject, as you teach concepts and topical lessons that can be understood by children who are close in age.

Grouping similar ages and concept-based subjects together saves time and motivates children to engage on a group learning level in discussion and collaborative assignments. Science experiments are more exciting to do together. History timelines are easily learned by any age and can be more engaging when learning those lessons through music, art projects, or hands-on shared activities. Whether you are reading a science unit study, preparing microscope slides, painting Van Gogh's *Starry Night*, or listening to your most recent read-aloud and doing dictation work together, all four motions are simultaneously happening.

Your home does not need to stop functioning because of this group learning time. There will be older, independent students who need a quiet space during this motion for a research paper, math work, or other more concentrated learning. There may be a baby napping or lunch being prepared by another child, all while this motion or any other motion is in progress.

Group learning affords you the gift of time. Your presence is not needed to teach younger students every core subject individually. Take advantage of grouping similar ages, young or old, to fit in the subjects that work well for this example, and to add in the special hands-on learning fun that bring their books to life. This is a great space to utilize the time of this motion for those experiments, art projects, flashcard contests, letter writing exercises, and your creative supplemental ideas that you worry you'll never have time for.

Use this motion wisely. It doesn't have to look the same every day. Rotate your group learning topics to ensure you are choosing what is the best for each week.

*Motion Four: Individual Seatwork*

This will be the most challenging motion for your children. Some will cherish the independence, but a few may need more accountability during this motion to complete their assignment. It may take some work to teach your child how to work independently, focusing on efficiency and responsibility. Give them the tools to avoid distractions and to work within a time limit you have set up for them.

During this motion, your children who are not engaged in group work, practicing, chores, or helping a sibling will be seated in the same area where you can always see them. They should work quietly and stay focused, using neatness, diligence, and attentiveness during this motion. You may think there is no way they will sit without you standing over them or helping them. It can be done, friends. Remember, the effort invested in your plan will be the most work. All our children should learn to be still, quiet, and independent in their working spaces. They will learn respect for others' time and accountability for their own personal space and time.

When my children came across a problem or question in their individual seatwork, I instructed them prior to this motion to circle the problems for later or to try again. Or when we had our one-on-one time after lunch, I would sit and help them with those problems. This kept their work in motion, avoided multiple interruptions, and gave each child the peace of mind that they were not on their own for their work, a feeling that can lead to frustration and apathy.

When the four motions are working simultaneously, the work is getting done. Everyone is doing something different, yet at the same time, with no idleness or restless children standing over your shoulder waiting for their "turn" with you or disappearing into their rooms or outside because you aren't available. The wonderful peace (and piece) in this plan is knowing you are hitting the benchmarks for your child's individual goals and specific interests. From responsibilities, academics, study habits, and personal goals to growth, character, independence, and more, your family will learn to work as a team as you go through the motions together. You may be the manager, but you're not the only one capable of being responsible for the many tasks that need to get done.

## TOOLS FOR TEACHING MULTIPLES

My husband is a builder, and I am always amazed at the speed and proficiency with which he can finish a project. He tells me it is his tools, and I know, yes, it is partly because of his tools, but mainly because he is a craftsman and has grown skilled at using the tools and learning the trade. He uses big power tools for each of his jobs, but when he is at home and we have minor needs like replacing a battery or tightening a doorknob, he uses the best tool known to man—the multitool. It folds up and has many purposes. He carries this on his work belt and always has it handy. I even have my own multipurpose tool but keep mine in the silverware drawer (because that is where moms keep everything that is indispensable, right?). It's where we need it when we need it.

A toolbox of learning tools will be the number #1 best thing you will ever have for your homeschooling journey. I have a go-to mental and physical checklist that I use for aids in grading, learning levels, troubleshooting, seasons of many or few, group studies, one-on-one, fun learning, and individual learning styles. These are tools you will have handy and readily available when you need support, a fill-in, or a new idea or approach.

On our school table, I keep a small bin of frequently used multi-purpose learning aids. I can reach for addition or sight-word cards, small practice clocks for telling time, and dry erase markers and small handheld white boards for dictation practice. I include fidget toys, small rulers, a red pen, dice, sticker packs for fun rewards, and motivational items that I want to have handy for accessibility. This saves me time and aids me in more effective teaching. I keep a three-tiered rolling cart next to me that holds larger teaching tools, such as special learning binders I have created with sheet protectors for use with dry erase markers.

Usually, one binder can include general topics for continuous review. From math facts, map labeling, months of the year, handwriting, and sight words to name a few, your binder can be created with your student needs in mind. This teaching tool can be used to keep one student busy if you are working with another student. Your rolling cart can hold larger, frequently needed items.

Don't reinvent the wheel when it comes to new ways of teaching or filling time with your multiples just to keep everyone happy. Your children will be learning while enjoying the spaces you need to fill in gaps. Look at this list as the multitool in your kitchen drawer, available when you need a new idea or approach, a fix-it for the moment, or a new way for teaching a concept your children are struggling to learn. I have these available and ready to "pull out" almost daily when I feel the strain, sense the kids' boredom and moodiness, or see someone has a gap in their motions and is disrupting the homeschool flow. Preemptive plans are going to be more helpful to you than reactive plans.

Below are the kinds of hands-on tools and time savers you might include in your toolkit:

### Hands-On Tools

- Computers: keyboarding, self-paced courses, researching current events
- Group study kits: unit studies, science or art projects, busy or sensory boxes
- Binders with laminated sheets for morning seatwork and review
- Flashcards
- Books of the Bible cards and memory work, math facts, phonics review cards for review and studying
- Independent worksheets
- Art corners and mini science stations
- Memory work: flashcards, binders, mapping (fill-in-the-blank with sheet protectors for repetitive use and independent work)
- Laminated chore charts with visuals and clear chore instructions
- Maps and laminated review sheets for geography
- Classic readers and phonics basics for daily review

### Time-Saving Tips

- Rotate days of the week for certain subjects; not every subject needs to be done every day
- Group studies
- Share responsibilities

- Set up a buddy system
- Mix teaching elements to meet learning styles and pique interest
- Create stations with activities parallel to your studies
- Create play and learning stations for younger children for busy learning and hands-on work
- Set goals per month, week, and day per quarter per child
- Lessons and errands on the same day to avoid and minimize distractions
- Time off
- Outsourcing and help

## TRADING TOOLS FOR TIME

There are many days when you will have a desperate need for something other than a solution, a new schedule, or an antidote for making it all work. Time will be your worst enemy and your best friend. When you feel time working against you, use the motions and tools we discussed; and on the days where you want to roll with it, use time as your friend and do the life together you dreamed of when you chose to homeschool.

Not only is it useful to clock the hours in learning with your children, but it is vital (and life-giving in every sense of the word) for you to find the time daily in a quiet space focusing on the life-giving Word and with the God who sees you in the crowded and big life you are living. There will be days when the walls of your home will feel like they are closing in on you. The noise will be deafening, the fridge will seem bare, and you haven't found a quiet, free minute alone in what seems to be forever.

Homeschooling many children is going to refine you, remake you, and renew a deeper faith and trust in Jesus than ever before. It is a given. Because if it doesn't, then you will find yourself overwhelmed, hopeless, tired, and not able to see, know, or finish the homeschooling seasons with joy. Spiritual disciplines in our own lives are tools for an abundant life. The overflow of abundance is where the joy in homeschooling many children will come from. Otherwise, you will easily fall into the trap of being a foreman on the job, managing all the pieces like it is a business. Then, any joy, identity, or relationship you had with the Lord and with your children will become a very small piece of your homeschooling.

Walk with me for a minute as I step out onto my porch in the middle of the movement of my home—the home that gives life to my children and their education, but where I am feeling the most alone that I ever have. I can hear the gravel under my feet as I force each step to just walk away from the house on purpose. The buddy system is active, and everyone is safe, busy, watched over, and working. I have absolutely no reason to be hovering and always teaching, cleaning, correcting, or doing the homeschool mom jobs. It is okay for me to step away and take a walk.

I am enjoying the quiet and solitude. It is so foreign to me that the silence seems deafening; I barely recognize my own thoughts. Thoughts of my child's struggles, dinner prep, bills to pay, curriculum choices, college forms, and toddler sleeping woes consume my thought patterns. I force my feet to stop mid-stride and to pray out loud. I need to hear the words and not just think them: "I am here, Lord. Stepping away to hear Your voice. Each step is like a walk toward You and the quieting of my heart and soul. I can hear my breath under the labor of my pace, and it is a reminder to me of Your presence as I exhale praise with each stride. This feels like freedom, and I can feel the weight falling off my shoulders as I see your strength in creation all around me. You have cared for me so deeply and provided me with all I need. This silence allows me to remember all You have done and will continue to do. I needed this time. Help me to steward the rest of my day to point my children to the reminders You have given me today."

*········ personal reflection ········*

Where do I need to change routines and schedules to keep everyone on track and foster more independent learners? Does my family function well as a team?

*········ personal challenge ········*

Time is your friend when you spend it wisely. Fostering a relationship with Jesus with your time is the most life-giving, life-sustaining gift. It is our primary job to steward our time in spiritual disciplines to find the abundant life in the middle of homeschooling many. This can look like taking a walk; making space in your day where you can close your bedroom door and sit in the stillness and talk with Jesus; and praying before you rise or worshiping during school together. These are of course simple and small check-ins to the most valuable time a busy homeschool mom can carve in to restore her soul.

*········ drawing from the well ········*

It is easy to become the doer of all things in our homeschool worlds. We tend to create a system that works for some and not for all. Our inner survival and caregiver mode has us at the center of the wheel and we can become overwhelmed and reactive. Homeschooling multiple children will be a full-time job, but God has equipped you with everything you need. The tools and ideas you create and use are a helpful supplement to the strength and care God has for you.

*"But he said to me, 'My grace is sufficient for you, for my power is made perfect in weakness.' Therefore I will boast all the more gladly of my weaknesses, so that the power of Christ may rest upon me."*
2 Corinthians 12:9

---- *a prayer for my homeschool* ----

Father God, my head is full of this busy, full life and I want to be present with You in the quiet right here and now. Help me silence the voices so I can be present with You now. I am in desperate need of Your promises before me as I walk. Help me love my kids well, homeschool with joy, and remember that not everything depends on me. I am tired, lonely, and in desperate need of reminders of who I am. Help me remember who You say I am. Fill me with Your presence as I take these next steps here and at home. I trust You. I need You. I am walking in faith and asking for a new and fresh vision for this day. In Jesus' name, Amen.

*chapter 7*

- - - •• - • - - - - - •••

# Learning to Pivot

*I*f you have come this far in your homeschooling, you have come a long way in knowing and believing you *can* homeschool . . . and most likely are doing it well. The secret to starting strong and knowing you are going to be okay is in these three little words: Plan. Pivot. Pace. We will unfold the importance of your pace in the next chapter.

These words will be your best friends every time you become stuck, doubtful, overwhelmed, or feel like giving up. I keep them in mind daily, and not only does my homeschool start and stay strong because of them, but so do my home, my personal life, and my approach to most anything worthy of my investment. Write them down in your planner. Understand what they will mean to you and memorize them before you move forward in your journey with grace.

Our first twenty years of marriage were like a marathon at full speed without any breaks. My husband and I learned the art of passing the baton to each other when we hit the wall, and we mastered the art of seamlessly handing off the responsibilities of our home to one another with care and precision. If we planned carefully, we could manage our household with amazing teamwork. This was our plan and it worked well, until we chose homeschooling, and I was the only runner training for this race. With our single income family and the work hours my husband needed to put in so we could homeschool, I was holding the baton daily with no one to pass it off to. Sometimes, the race isn't what we are training for, but the stamina and ability to enter the race. Homeschooling would get the best of me if I didn't plan. My home had a plan, my schedule had a plan, my kids had a plan, and I was going to need some training to do this well.

There are some days that change you. Days when there is no one to pass the baton to and you are up to your eyeballs in life, and you know something must change. One morning, as I served the kids breakfast, cleaned up the baby, set the littles up with their toys, and asked the older kiddos to bring their school crates to the kitchen table, I realized the four older kids were missing and probably off on another great adventure to avoid bookwork. I felt defeated, knowing how much time it would take to re-create this moment when the younger kids were set, and we could "fit in" our schoolwork. By the time I found them, I discovered the two oldest boys had dared their younger brother to climb onto the flat roof of our single-story home. He'd accepted. I arrived at the scene to find him running the length of the roof, laughing to the cheers of his older brothers and sister.

I coaxed him to the edge as calmly as I could. He had gotten up there by climbing a nearby tree and jumping onto the edge of the roof, but coming down would be better on the ladder I found in the garage. So I was the lucky one to hoist him down and rescue him from this daring adventure. Of course, this story completely leaves out my management and safe care of my kiddos inside, the baby sleeping, and the toddlers who were by now outside watching this escapade. Add in the lecture and the family meeting at the end of this truth-or-dare school hour and you can imagine just how much "school" we got done on that day. This became one of the days in my homeschooling repertoire marked as "needing a plan."

I would love to tell you this was a one-time event and every day since then we have operated like a well-oiled machine. But I cannot tell you this because planning for our homeschool means we also plan for the unexpected. We learn to pivot when necessary and remember life is oblivious to our schedules and a non-respecter of our plans.

If you want to start strong and finish well, plan and learn to pivot.

## FLEXIBILITY WILL BE YOUR FRIEND

"Pivot" is my number one life word as a homeschool mama. This word has given me permission to make a change when nothing is going according to plan. I have learned to pivot at the start of the day, in the middle of curriculum, and during spontaneous changes when everyone is having a bad day. As a former Type A personality, I needed time to practice and to see the benefits of pivoting in my home and homeschooling.

Learning to pivot trades in perfection for flourishing.

How do you know it's a good time to pivot? You may be surprised to find you've already pivoted many times in your homeschooling and done it well. Look at the list below and identify which "pivots" you've experienced and managed well. Which ones could you plan to better pivot for next time? What items would you add?

- Schedule hasn't allowed for good rest
- Learning is lackluster
- Unexpected company or errands
- Sickness
- Appointments take longer than usual
- Stir crazy and the four walls seem like they are closing in
- What you are doing isn't working
- Friend plans are rare, and you receive an invite
- Child is struggling to focus, and you don't want to lose a whole day of learning
- One subject is taking too much time
- Beautiful weather you don't want to miss
- _____
- _____

## LEARNING THE ART OF PIVOTING

Learning to pivot will take work. Pivoting is not "just" putting the books away and stepping away for a break. Pivoting is not changing curriculums and approaches whenever something is hard or not working. As you homeschool daily, it is good to practice small pivots, preparing for the moments guaranteed to come.

Homeschooling requires focus, and as a mom of many children, distraction was my number one nemesis to overcome to accomplish a full day of work.

On multiple occasions, we have experienced severe winter weather where we live that has caused whiteouts and loss of electricity and heat. To avoid having these situations disrupt our school day in the future, we purchased small gas heaters. Usually, a power outage is an adventure, given that we know the electric company is on the job. Most of the time, we sleep through these outages, go to town, or wait it out. But the time we experienced a string of long days without heat, my super ninja pivot powers came in handy. Everyone wore extra pairs of socks, layers of clothing, and even winter hats, and we made a big pivot. We gathered our books, the portable heaters, snacks, and water bottles, and we homeschooled in my bedroom. We set up stations around my room, on my bed, still getting our work done for the day.

On other days, the atmosphere in our schoolroom has been mind-numbingly quiet. While I am so proud of everyone for showing up and giving their best, I choose to surprise them and pivot with an unscheduled break. I tell the kids to put their work down and grab their shoes and water bottles because we are going for a one-hour hike and an ice cream cone, on the condition that afterward we will dive back into our work without complaining. After a loud cheer from everyone, we make a mental and physical pivot, create a lasting memory, and come back to finish strong.

When it comes to fitting in enrichment activities for my children, I have chosen to pivot strong when I see an opportunity. Often, we will be in the middle of our homeschool morning and I know we need to break out of the four walls of our home. As I instruct them to wrap up their work independently, I quietly and quickly slip away to pack a simple lunch, refill the diaper bag, grab our paints and paper, and let them all know we are headed to the lake to skip rocks and eat our lunch. While we are there, I have them each pick a spot to sit with their lunch and set up their paints and paper for painting their chosen perspective. What a glorious pivot, accomplishing much more than a painting activity. We were able to breathe in God's creation, each having a space of quiet and retreat. We got out of the house and were also an example of home-schooling to those around us.

There will be days when groceries, library returns, music lessons, and playground visits take over your academic hours and you men-tally pivot to doubling up lessons the day prior or the days after. The unexpected visitors at your door call for a physical pivot to extend hospitality and reinforce your kids' independent seatwork time. When a few of your children wake up sick and your attention is needed for comfort and care, you may homeschool from the couch with your sick child on your lap and your other children moving like chess pieces in between you and independent learning.

## PRACTICE YOUR PIVOT EARLY

When you consider the word "pivot," think about an actual men-tal and physical turning in another direction. Take what is already happening and seemingly out of your control and move away from the situation into another direction for the moment or day, the child, or maybe even your homeschool approach. Take the best and leave the rest.

Don't lose hope if you are feeling stuck. Sometimes, it is so much easier if someone else gives us the nudge to make a change. We get stuck in the lists, the planner, the schedule, the "this is homeschooling," and we end up in a spiral of frustration, fear, and discouragement. Pivoting doesn't mean walking away from the very thing that isn't working. Pivoting is like putting a pin in the moment, considering a slight move that will accomplish the better good, and taking the lessons with us.

Learning to pivot early on will be a lifesaver in your homeschool journey—for you and for your children. The top two tips in learning to be a pro-pivoter are 1) learning to recognize potential roadblocks before they happen, and 2) knowing how you would normally respond in those circumstances. There have been so many instances when I became completely derailed from change or a need for a change in our homeschool. Once I learned to process the changes as little speedbumps and not roadblocks, I was able to pivot well. This is now a natural mindset and shift for me to make. Pivoting well has not only made my homeschool better for all of us, but it has also been good for my mental and physical health. I'm better able to love fully, be present, and not feel shut down by the normal stresses that come along with homeschooling.

*........ personal reflection ........*

Have I set a plan we can live with, and do I have habits of flexibility and the ability to pivot well? Where can I reset our homeschool journey to reflect commitment, flexibility, and a pace we can all live with?

*........ personal challenge ........*

I will begin making a practice of planning well and learning to pivot where needed. I will practice flexibility and make the best of the moments out of my control.

I will:

1. Consider the current challenging circumstance and focus on a solution.
2. Focus on my child and their needs above the homeschool plan.
3. Work with what I have and make the very best of it.
4. Take our homeschool work with us, wherever the pivot takes us.
5. Try doing the same thing in a different way.
6. Tell my kids a change of plans is not a big deal, and we all need a new and fresh perspective.
7. Remember not all pivots have to be big.
8. Homeschool in a different room or at a different time for the day.
9. Homeschool one child at a time for a day.
10. Not get stuck in a rut that leaves me so deeply discouraged I can't see my way out.
11. Ask others for fresh and new ideas.
12. Use the word "pivot" in my home so my children learn to be adaptable and flexible.

13. Learn the same things in new ways.
14. Assign and reassign jobs and chores.
15. Create an environment of consistency, so when I make a change, my mind rests in knowing I am doing the work.
16. Run my household with steady rhythms, so when I make a change, everything else stays the same.
17. Stay true to our homeschool vision, and remind myself that a pivot is a positive turn with continuous, positive momentum.
18. Identify our reactions to change and consider the when, where, and how I chose to pivot.

## drawing from the well

Don't worry about your pace as much as your purpose in your pace. We can find hope in knowing that by leaning into the work God has set before us, we will reap a harvest. Working unto ourselves and a fast-paced, ill-defined schedule will lead to discouragement.

*"Commit to the LORD whatever you do,*
*and he will establish your plans."* Proverbs 16:3 NIV

## a prayer for my homeschool

Lord, I commit our daily homeschool hours to You. Help me to live in surrender to the plan You have for each of us and for the capacity within us all. In Jesus' name, Amen.

*part two*

# Stay
# the
# Course

"Do not let the endless succession of small things
crowd great ideals out of sight and out of mind."[2]

**CHARLOTTE MASON**

2. Sonya Shafer, "What Everybody Ought to Know About Choosing Curriculum and Schedules," Simply Charlotte Mason, https://simplycharlottemason.com/blog/what-everybody-ought-to-know-about-choosing-curriculum-and-schedules.

*chapter 8*

- - - ● - ● ● - ● ● - - - ● ● ●

# Slow and Steady

*W*hen I go to the beach with our children, everything we will need is packed tightly into our red, bent-handled beach wagon. I think every American family owns one, and if not, has witnessed the dramatic and entertaining scenes of others transporting the heavy, overloaded wagons across the beach to the water and back. Entertaining, because I have been on both the pulling and observing ends of this event. The long haul is not a quick or rushed process. With the wagon handle between our two-handed grip, our fingers laced behind our back, our sandals off because they are a hindrance, we lean forward and decide this is the moment.

It doesn't take very long for us to realize the sand is hot beneath our feet, and as hurried as we want to make this happen, the wagon's weight, the large bulky wheels, the wandering children, and the well-organized and packed wagon has a mind of its own on the sinking sand. Every few feet, something else falls out and needs to be restacked, and the stops and starts mean a new decision to breathe in patience and keep moving forward. Running is not an option. Impatience gets us nowhere good. Stopping and restarting help readjust the load. And it is obvious everyone is watching and counting on you. I call this the long haul: we look to the end goal, choose our destination, and know it is time to lean in and pull.

Hitting the sand in full motion is great for the novice, but the experienced have learned to plan for the slow and steady crawl to reach the destination.

Learning "slow and steady" is a skill. One worth observing, practicing, and perfecting. This beach image will stick with you through your homeschool journey, when you feel rushed, overwhelmed, underwhelmed, and cannot see the finish line. The pace we set now will determine how we finish and how we succeed in the process. The homeschool "wagon" is piled high and overflowing, all with great intentions and careful consideration, but moving it will still be a haul. In fact, there is more to carry than what is in the wagon, all while we are doing our best to delegate and shift the weight.

There are always options to every scenario. We may have to ask someone to lift the other end of the wagon and help us carry it, forgetting the wheels and the plan we had before. We can plan to have someone push, while we pull from the lead. The choice to make the load lighter and relegate splitting the weight between everyone always makes things easier.

The slow and steady pace will bring us to the perfect spot we chose ahead of time. Along the way, we may need to go slower, or sometimes, a little faster—we can decide. The momentum and strength are all in the pulling. The determination and the tiny decisions along the way enable us to do it all over again at the end of the day. Repacking the wagon with your tired people and calling them up to finish the journey back across the sand is your job once again. The wagon has served you well, so you steward it. You clean it out, you pack it up, you make sure it is ready when you need it. Because you are the steward of your time and your resources.

The reward is in the arriving. We know there will be a time of rest at the end of the long haul if we have planned and paced ourselves well. The exhaustion may still be real, the tasks won't disappear, but if we allow ourselves time to enjoy the rewards of our work, then it is worth it. When we fail to plan, hurry ourselves, our children, and the process, push from behind, rather than leading and pulling with patience, we will feel the strain, the frustration, and eventually, the defeat.

*Homeschooling requires a slow and steady pace to the finish line— a patient pursuit of strategy, perseverance, strength, and a sustainable pace that works for everyone.*

## SETTING A SUSTAINABLE PACE

We all have varying capacities, and no race is run the same way. Know your pace and how you function best as a homeschool mom. Some of you read the beach wagon analogy and were able to troubleshoot, simplify, and discount the burden of it from the beginning of my story. Some of you read the scenario, nodding your head in agreement and acknowledgment that this has been and would be you. For some of us, we've been there, done that, and adjusted with experience and wisdom to pivot from a wagon to a backpack and the whole team is on board. There is not a right way or a wrong way; embrace your pace and take it slow and steady.

We are not in a race against one another or against time. Often, we hurry ourselves and our children with timers, demands, and frustration over a slower pace, as we watch what the world is doing and how fast life is going by. And do—dare I ask—we sometimes feel like we are missing out? We set a pace to meet the ideal plan in the least amount of time and our pace is not for the benefit of our children, but for us. In the end, this is not sustainable.

Homeschooling is a sacrifice, and when we feel deterred because of time and frustrated by slow starts and lagging lessons that carry into our own plans, we forget our true assignment: showing up.

*The hurried homeschooler leaves no time for routine,*
*perseverance, and sustainability.*

Your pace must be not only sustainable for you, but must benefit your children's ability to learn and not have your home crumble around you. Here are a few areas to focus on to ensure your homeschool pace is slow and steady.

### Commitment

For the busy homeschooler, the "doer," a set-in-stone schedule or days waiting on the hard-to-learn lessons to be completed can be absolutely infuriating. These will be some of the challenges to keeping a steady pace. If you find yourself frustrated with waiting for that last child to finish their lessons, or you feel homeschooling is "getting in the way of everything else," perhaps it isn't a lack of commitment, but a lack of keeping a steady pace.

Only you can make this happen. You are pulling the beach wagon with one hand and allowing those significant pieces to fall off one by one without noticing. Your commitment to a slower pace will lead to success. The end goal is worth adjusting the weight and considering how to reset and steady the load you are carrying—before it gets away from you.

## Consistency

Showing up to do the work at a steady pace is effectually more helpful to you and to your children. Eclectic, classical, unschooling methods aside, if we treat our children's learning styles with consistent commitment, it will reflect on not only their academics, but their personal character and work ethic as they grow. We are teaching them the importance of showing up regularly and making our homeschooling a priority in our daily rhythms.

Create routines that work for your family. Make your morning gathering time a nonnegotiable and uninterrupted time. Set your teaching schedule per child and subjects to a consistent daily schedule. Avoid the mindset of "fitting it in, or "making it work." Consistency thrives with commitment and our children thrive with clear expectations.

## Capacity

You will quickly learn your capacity and adapt your schedule and pace accordingly. Sometimes we first experience a learning curve, balls dropping, overload, or gaps in our homeschooling outcome before we adjust and readjust accordingly. Two main checkmarks I give myself in this area are: 1) Are we maintaining a steady rhythm and showing up regularly? and 2) Are we getting our work done at a pace that enables us to reach our goal?

Showing up to do a little work on a regular basis is better than giving up and not doing it at all. You may consider covering some school subjects only twice a week and core subjects daily. This provides attention to the necessary lessons but allows you to invest more capacity (time and attention) to the most fundamental subjects. Choose the most pertinent areas of your homeschool and give them the most time and energy, while creating small spaces for everything else. Once you find a consistent rhythm, you will be able to clearly choose what and when you can add more. Your capacity will actually grow with the ease of your consistent schedule.

## BURDEN OR BLESSING

Part of a successful homeschool pace is determined by our attitudes and actions. Our attitude usually dictates how much time we give to something. When we show up to a homeschooling day with other things on our mind, and we see the schoolwork as drudgery or in anticipation to get to the next thing, I can guarantee everyone will feel your hurriedness. Similarly, a consistent pace and commitment to the nonnegotiables may also feel annoying and "in the way."

I have discovered my attitude often dictates how I teach my children. There will be days you just don't want to show up and take it slow and steady. In those moments, I recommend choosing what is best and leaving the rest. Give those areas your 100 percent best attitude and pace the work to avoid a rushed lesson.

Our attitude toward homeschooling is vital to success. A homeschooling mama who sees her job as an inconvenience will cause her children to feel hurried in their work. When they need more guidance or they struggle with a concept, their first instinct will be to not burden or bother with asking for help. Their attitude antennae are strong.

I learned the hard way. In order to fit everything in, there were days I rushed the kids through their lessons and on to the next thing. The hurried pace didn't allow me to relax and be present. This affected my mood and my stress level and left my kids completely frazzled. Homeschooling became a burden on the days I had failed to set a sustainable schedule and pace. Learning to schedule piano lessons, errands, and any extracurricular activities on the same day allowed me to enjoy uninterrupted days of learning at home. The blessing in my homeschooling came from me knowing how much homeschooling was working for my children and me. When I began feeling the stress and the hurriedness, it quickly felt like a burden to us all. I found the best way to preserve the sacredness of enjoying our homeschooling was to "savor the slow" and set a sustainable pace for the rest. This applies to our schedules, our choices, our attitudes. If we are in too big of a hurry, we miss the blessings.

*······· personal reflection ·······*

What do my children see in me when I show up to homeschool each day? What am I racing against and feeling pressure from?

*······· personal challenge ·······*

I will set my pace to slow and steady and eliminate the hurry from our home and school.

*······· drawing from the well ·······*

When we rise, as we walk and as we rest, may we remember to clothe ourselves in the hope we have in Jesus and what *He* has called us to. His hope is transferable, and this is what we want our children to see and know of us as we show up every day to teach them.

> *"Put on then, as God's chosen ones, holy and beloved, compassionate hearts, kindness, humility, meekness, and patience."*
> Colossians 3:12

*···· a prayer for my homeschool ····*

Lord, help me keep my eyes steadfastly focused on You. Help me avoid going ahead of Your plan and pace for us. You are the giver of peace, and I am reminded of Your power and might. Help my focus to be set on the time I have with my children daily. I want our home to thrive and our pace to be one of peace and productivity. You are sufficient for all of my needs. Help me find You in the busyness and the work. In Jesus' name, Amen.

*chapter 9*

# Triggers and Traps

was talking to my daughter-in-law about areas of my home-schooling and my motherhood that I realized had become, simply put, "triggers." I discovered homeschooling triggers to be scenarios or experiences that provoked a definite response. Over the years, I have recognized similar triggers or responses in other homeschooling mamas. Noticing these during my earlier years of homeschooling would have helped me find solutions sooner.

I found that most of my triggers were emotional, and the traps I fell into were rooted in my physical or spiritual life. I would feel stuck at home (physically), and this would lead into a time of loneliness. When I put in hours of effort and energy to home-school, I was physically taxed, and my children's laziness would trigger an emotional response. Recognizing our own triggers and traps is helpful in navigating our responses and cultivating a healthy homeschool.

While in the thick of my homeschooling journey, I was also rais-ing a growing family and living a life of ministry in and with my family. Various circumstances made homeschooling feel isolating, challenging, and difficult. I originally hesitated to write this chapter with this title. But if there is one thing I have learned from homeschooling, writing, and using my stories for the glory of God, it is knowing where I can lean in the most to encourage you where you are. It would be remiss of me to leave out the hard stories and seasons of my experience and only offer you advice and lists. That is not who I am. Hard is not bad. Hard is hard, and from those things, we can grow to be better, stronger, and more reliant on a Savior who gives us the hope of the gospel, where He meets us daily.

Homeschooling can be lonely, challenging, and financially straining. It can add an unneeded layer of stress to our homes and relationships if we are not careful. Below are triggers I have experienced and witnessed in other homeschooling families.

Talking about them will help ensure other mamas are not blindly walking in unhealthy patterns today. My purpose is to encourage you to stay alert to these ruts and patterns, keep your mind stayed on Christ, and keep our focus centered on His precepts daily. Remember, this is my story too. You are not alone.

*Stuck*

This is a big trap and all too familiar to most homeschoolers. Sadly, being stuck is also a big secret. The problem is, no one really knows how stuck you are (or were) and will never know because, in the big homeschooling and social media world, who wants to be "the one" with the struggles? None of us wants to be the one to stand up at the annual homeschooling conferences and share, "I am stuck and want to get out," or "I feel confined, trapped, and need space."

This is where we experience shame. Sometimes, we convince

ourselves this is normal, that we will survive, or that we must not be called to homeschooling because everyone else seems just fine and content. Sadly, shame is often inflicted on us by others in the homeschool community. Whether on purpose or through our own comparison, feeling stuck can cause feelings of shame that can lead to isolation.

Feeling stuck can begin with looming questions or a child with learning struggles you haven't figured out how to reach. You may feel as though you don't have friends or a social life anymore. You are home day after day without a break, waiting on your child's learning timeline, waiting on the multiple children to rotate through their schedules, waiting for your husband to get home, waiting for the car, waiting for the free moment to simply take a walk. You feel trapped in a world that seems to have no room for you—and too embarrassed to ask for a free moment, to ask how to fix this, or to tell someone how lonely homeschooling can be because you fear you are in the minority.

First and foremost, calling out the issue can be the best place to free yourself. I will be the first to raise my hand and say, yes, this was me, and I regret never noticing how deeply trapped I had become. I became ensnared to loneliness and thinking this "was just the way it was." Many days I gave up trying to find a solution. I stopped looking for opportunities to have free time. I didn't ask for help or solutions, and my space felt smaller and smaller each day. What began as a wide-open opportunity of freedom to choose our schedules and have the time we needed to enrich our lives with homeschooling became a narrow space I felt trapped in.

The only way to break free from feeling stuck is to move. On a rare and special trip to visit my dear friend, author Sally Clarkson, I saw the world through a new lens. As she and I were talking late one evening, she asked me what I do when I am not homeschooling my children. My answer came in a fresh flow of tears. In her wisdom, she folded my hands in hers and challenged me to find five women I could reach out to when I was feeling stuck or lonely and five ways to get out of this trap and to move into new and fulfilling areas for my life.

When I returned home, I began praying for those five women. I began walking every day (movement), started a new homeschool co-op and a women's Bible study, and scheduled a weekly date night with my husband—no excuses. The best way to get unstuck is to move, and sometimes we need the nudge from a loving friend. Take the next steps, friends. There is hope on the other side.

## Negativity

This is both a trap and a trigger. If you spent time with me or around my children, you would hear me say just how "ugly" negativity looks and sounds. I call this a trap because it is a "small" bad habit in our homes that can potentially grow until we find ourselves captive to it. Negativity can be the way we communicate, the way we operate, and a way of life. Whining, laziness, ungratefulness, and complaining are all negative traps we may be walking into, unaware of the impact they have on our homeschooling mindset. Negativity can quickly change the tone of a day and become intertwined with our thinking, teaching, and our kids' learning. Its tentacles reach far beyond the doors of our home.

Not only is negativity in all its forms a trap, but it can be a silent trigger to the homeschool mom who has selflessly and seriously thrown herself into her role as the primary educator. This homeschooler seeks wisdom and has learned to celebrate her wins and learn from her losses. She has faced struggles and asked for help; she has experienced defeat and hard, lonely days, but she has found her people. She has learned to lean into wisdom and give 100 percent to her home and to herself, knowing the payoff will far outweigh the learning curve. If this is you, negativity may be a trigger for you.

A whining or ungrateful child may tip your day in the wrong direction. A child's complaining or lazy spirit could create a negative emotion or reaction you would identify as justified or sacrificial on your part; therefore, you expect reciprocation. You are triggered when you hear non-homeschooling moms complain about how hard and long summer days can be with their children. You may be triggered when you hear public school parents complain about the rights their students should have, and you are triggered when our family is complacent about the opportunities you have given them.

The best way to combat negativity is to avoid comparison and remind yourself that this is the path you chose, and you are content in the choices you are making.

*Pride*

I didn't want to write about this homeschooling trap, but pride is one some homeschooling families fall into. We might begin to think our child's education is without fault or homeschooling is "the only way" or "superior" to any other form of education. When we become so proud of our choice to homeschool and our children grow up in a "we are better than they are" culture, we are elevating our choice to homeschool and the quality of education our children have above others.

I included this trap because, as much as pride often exists in the homeschooling world, there is a way out and a better way—homeschooling laced with humility and graced with His presence. When our homeschooling becomes about us, it is our way and not God's way. This trap is dangerous and deep and there can be lasting effects. But we can avoid this trap by guarding our steps and listening well to wisdom. There are many benefits to listening and *hearing*. I've often asked my kids, "I know you are telling me you are listening, but do you really hear what I am saying?" There is a difference, right?

In the trap of pride, we may discover we are either not listening, or we dismiss the value of another's opinion. Or we are listening but not hearing the truth of their words. Pride will sink us and bring us low. It feels good and creates the illusion that we are in control. I can tell you from experience that below the surface of pride lurks insecurity and a lack of respect, honor, or humility. One of the symptoms of this painful trap in our homeschooling is the "we can do no wrong" mentality. Symptoms include misbehaving children and children who aren't learning. They suffer similar symptoms to ours: lack of respect and honor, and the mindset that homeschoolers are supreme.

God has given us discernment, and when we learn to exercise this and apply it to our lives, we are able to weigh valid points and truth, convert them into action, and climb out of this trap. Or avoid it altogether.

## Laziness

There is a difference between the weary homeschooler and the lazy homeschooler. I would never give another person this label, but laziness is a trap I often caution others about and challenge myself to stay alert to the symptoms and dangers of this in our own homeschooling. Laziness is a default reaction to overwhelmingly difficult schedules, struggles with finances or family, or a lack of accountability, and sadly at times, a pure lack of effort. Laziness is a comfortable trap for some homeschooling families. It can reflect the culture of our homes or can be exhibited by one child who brings a lackadaisical effort to their work. This trap has ripple effects on their learning, reviews, assessments, and application in other areas of life. Lazy homeschooling families are often half-committed and have chosen homeschooling as an alternative approach yet are not fully engaged or prepared.

This trap is also a trigger to the committed homeschooling family. Not everyone is prepared for the commitment, but the way to avoid this trigger or get out of this trap is to learn, study, ask for help, be diligent, and set up accountability checks, assessments, or a measure of progress.

Being diligent is probably the best antidote to falling behind, letting too many tasks go undone, not managing your time, and not setting homeschooling as a priority. Is being lazy easy to identify with? That's a sign you may be vulnerable to this trap. Traps cause pain. They can be deceiving, hidden from plain view, and can keep us from success. Avoid this trap by showing up, doing the work, and remaining committed.

## OUR BEST ANTIDOTE

What is the sovereignty of the Lord if we cannot place our trust in His plan and not fall into fear of the traps and triggers that catch us by surprise and ensnare us? Trusting in God's plan and His control will free us from the symptoms of pride, fear, laziness, and the overwhelming defeat we may feel when we walk out this homeschooling journey.

I would be remiss to not acknowledge the places of despair, the weaknesses, and the sin natures we all have and how they will show up and trap us in negative patterns, trying to defeat us after we've said yes to teaching our children. Acknowledging those very real and hard places allows us to recognize what we are experiencing and eventually find freedom.

······· *personal reflection* ·······

Does my personal homeschooling journey have areas I feel triggered by, or I feel trapped in? What are those areas? Is there someone I can reach out to help me in those areas?

······· *personal challenge* ·······

I will list the areas I find to be my (our) biggest homeschooling obstacles and challenges and find the root cause. I commit to working through each trigger and trap and will ask the Lord to be sovereign over all our homeschooling areas, including the challenges and aspects of homeschooling I do not necessarily like.

### Identifying Triggers and Traps

1. Am I homeschooling because I am worried what my friends would say if I didn't?
2. Do I rush my kids through their work with impatience?
3. Do I tell them how we are all waiting for them?
4. Have I ever left them to struggle alone while I move on with our day?
5. Do I watch the clock and feel resentment at the loss of personal time and my schedule?
6. Have I slowly isolated myself or my children because I find it too hard to fit it all in?
7. What are my words, attitudes, and approaches to our homeschooling work?
8. Do my children hear me complain about them, their work, homeschooling, and the effort and sacrifice it is for me?
9. Have I had a pattern of negative feedback about my children's behavior and am I working on this?
10. Do I think we are superior to those who don't homeschool? Do my children?

11. Do I skip lessons, subjects, or days because of time, preference, forgetfulness, and lack of prioritizing on a regular basis?

12. What is the first emotion I experience when someone asks me, "How is homeschooling going?" What are the first words I respond with when asked this question?

13. Do I feel annoyed and agitated when we give so much to homeschooling and encounter those who may not?

14. What triggers me the most in my personal homeschool space?

15. Do I see myself homeschooling beyond this year? If I don't have an answer, what thoughts about it come to mind?

──────── *drawing from the well* ────────

Trusting a sovereign God with our children, their education, our homes, and the homeschooling journey gives us permission to get out of our own way and walk in the Word, where He promises He will never leave us. God reassures us that His love remains constant even when we get stuck and need a way out. He commits to the journey with us when we turn it over to Him. The only way to stay the course is to trust the One who began a good work in us.

*"And whatever you do, whether in word or deed, do it all in the name of the Lord Jesus, giving thanks to God the Father through him."*
Colossians 3:17 NIV

──── *a prayer for my homeschool* ────

God, You know how I love the idea of homeschooling, and yet some days I am stuck, angry, and cannot see the future in any of this for me. Help me surrender my personal struggles and trust You. I am asking for perseverance, trust, and eyes to see the areas that have held us back and keep us from moving forward in joy. I trust You to make a way and for me to humbly lay my triggers and those traps I fall into at Your feet. In Jesus' name, Amen.

*chapter 10*

- - • • • - • - • - • • - •

# The Culture
# of My Home

*W*e all have a vision of what our homeschool should look like. We have ideas and ideals we've been mulling over and mindfully planning. We have considered schedules and our room set up, curriculum options, and how wonderfully freeing and stressfully limiting it could or will be. When it's all said and done, the number one impact and influence on your homeschooling will be the culture of your home. Your space will be special, but not as significant to your children as it is to you. Your schedule will keep you sane, and your curriculum will fluctuate and pivot with each child.

*Home is the most important and influential part of homeschool.*

## WHAT IS A "NORMAL" HOMESCHOOL DAY?

When I was in the thick of our homeschooling years, with six kiddos under the age of nine, I would choose a day of our homeschooling week when we focused on reading together, art projects, chores, exploring outdoors, and the benefits of being together with our own schedule. On those days, we would either stay in our jammies, dress up for a unit study themed day, put on our playclothes and spend time with the chickens, or go for nature walks in the woods. I'd never thought about the culture I was creating in our homeschool until someone asked me if they could shadow us during a normal homeschool day.

My mind quickly pictured what we do in a day. I was worried it wouldn't be interesting enough, scheduled enough, or quiet enough. The mental list continued to grow. Thankfully, our visitor enjoyed shadowing our family. But this visit caused me to think deeply about what exactly makes homeschooling unique and special. What makes us different if we are all using the same curriculum, making schedules, unschooling, or engaging in morning times, art lessons, and nature walks? I began to make note of the habits of our home and the repetitive motions and unique foundational pillars that made up our days. What makes our homeschooling different than "just school"? What would a stranger see if they stopped by unannounced or observed me without my knowing? These questions prompted me to begin considering the culture of my home. We have been given a responsibility and an amazing privilege to create and cultivate an environment of learning, but even more importantly, to steward the lives of our children.

When most people think of homeschooling, the main thought is "school at home." Life within the four walls of your home is just as important as their academics. Consider the seven "Ws" below as measures of the atmosphere of your home and the quality of life outside of your children's bookwork. Take a few moments with each "W," and think about how each sets the tone and culture in the life of your homeschooling.

## Words

There cannot be enough words in this book to emphasize the power of words in our homes and the lives of our children. Words can impact our children's identity and their outlook on life. Our words affect their ability to communicate through conflict. Words bring peace to a difficult day and encouragement to the struggling learner. Our tone sets our homeschool day in motion. Children can be motivated or discouraged by words. We have the power to shift an entire day with "just" our words.

This is so powerful! We are responsible to edify and encourage one another and to take responsibility for our words. Every day we have an opportunity to build up or tear down. Our words have impact. The power of the tongue can bring life. What do your words say to everyone within the four walls of your home? Are you teaching your children how to speak life to others?

I have found the most important lesson isn't always what I say, but how I say it. There are days when I feel as if I am on a continuous loop of asking my children to do the same task over and over until they get it right or listen to my instructions. As their frustration grows over the repetition, so does mine, and I find my tone changing from a simple request to a strained and stressed command. I have realized my children stop really listening at the point my voice changes and we are both at our limits. By this time, nothing of value is being communicated and nothing is really getting accomplished, other than a lot of stressful words and a strain to our relationship.

Isn't this how it goes, though? We try and help them with their math assignment, but the interaction can escalate into discouragement, impatience, and frustration. I have learned that when it comes to my words, I want my children to hear my request or the heart behind my words the first time. I ask myself what I want the final outcome to be before I speak. I may begin with something like this: "I am going to work with your sister on her spelling. You have some corrections to do on your math paper. I will go over one problem with you first and make sure you understand, and then I will set a ten-minute timer so you can try the rest on your own. If you have trouble, that's okay. I will help you, but I do expect you to try. I won't leave you upset about it. We will finish this together, but you must do what you can in the ten minutes, or I will not work with you until I see effort. I believe you can do this, okay? Do you understand? Let's try the first problem together."

This is a two-minute talk that sets up the next ten minutes to be conflict free. It avoids guesswork, raised voices, and unkind words. Our tone is just as important as the words we say. I want my homeschooling to be life-giving.

*Worship*

This is a large part of the homeschooling culture in our home. You may picture singing, Bible reading, studying in peace, and prayer at the beginning of every day. Yes, those are practices and habits we have implemented into our days, but there is a culture of homeschooling that weaves worship in and through our day. Worship as a culture of our homeschooling is an atmosphere of pointing everything back to our Creator. Worship dictates our words, our responses, our curriculum, and how and what we spend our time on.

Worship in our home always brings tears to my eyes. I see it as an outpouring of the fruit of the Spirit. On days when I had my hands full, rocking a sick baby, I could hear my daughters working with their siblings on their schoolwork or in the kitchen making breakfast. Their encouragement and praise were a sweet refrain to my ears as they filled in where needed and put on an attitude of praise. We have stopped our school day mid-stride to pray when we all realize one of us is having a bad day and everything seems hard or impossible.

We begin every morning together in worship. Only Jesus can take our weary hearts and give us a new perspective at the beginning of each new day. Waking up to simple songs and half-hearted singing usually moves us to compassion for one another as we show up to school a little tired and needing Jesus. Worship gets our own agenda out of the way.

Worship resets our attitudes because we are taking our eyes off ourselves.

Worship gives us words to the weary places and replaces discouragement with joy.

Worship invites us to remember our reason for homeschooling.

Worship points us back to the One who loves us the most.

## World

Often homeschooling families work extra hard to keep the world out of our homeschooling. I like to see it through the lens of "we get to choose when, how, and what" our children learn about the world when we are doing school and doing life. Our children need a biblical worldview, so they can be ready to compare the other worldviews they will encounter. The world is a big place and not all bad. I wanted my children to see the world with God's eyes for His people.

We taught our children how they will be faced with choices in and out of our home, but the safety net of our home would not always be there, so they needed to be aware, know, understand, and believe what their (our) worldview is. I often have this image of homeschooling families holding down the fort. Our homes are the foundation on which our children will build their knowledge and beliefs before "going into the world."

When one of my daughters got her driver's license at the age of sixteen, I asked her where she planned to go first. Her response took me a little by surprise. She had been planning what she called her "denomination project." She had a plan to visit local churches in every denomination, study their core beliefs and their worship and decide where she landed with her faith. We have always talked openly about different theologies and beliefs and the need for a solid foundation. She set a timeline of six months for this project. We watched with wide-eyed wonder and a little bit of concern as to where this might take her. She even invited me along once in a while. She learned a lot about faith, the world, and what she believed and why. After six months, she was at peace with where she needed to be, but more importantly, this experience gave her eyes to see others through the lens of humanity and how God sees us.

This was formative for her, and as scary as this could be to a mama's heart, I knew she had to do this because we had encouraged and taught our children to think and live this way while they grew up in our home.

## Wonder

When was the last time you closed your books and studied a topic of interest with your kids that wasn't on the syllabus? Wonder is an amazing motivator. It sparks invention and imagination. It invites spontaneity into the most structured homeschool. Wonder finds the golden nugget in the most boring of subjects or lessons. Encouraging wonder daily will be your gold-digging job as a homeschooling mom or parent. You will bring the ideas and watch them discover something exciting in even the most boring of subjects.

You will spot wonder in your children when they've excitedly spotted the tiniest monarch caterpillar munching a leaf in a field of milkweed. They'll carefully remove the leaf and carry it back to you in wide-eyed awe that it will soon become a beautiful butterfly.

Children were born with the sparkle of wonder. From watching the stems of dandelions curl in water to the chrysalis in the mason jar morph into a butterfly, their homeschooling eyes are opened to the Creator, His creation, and the wonder of how we learn. We have the same opportunity to wonder. Our reactions and interactions with wonder—their learning, their ideas, and their ingenuity—are just as important as "letting them" take the time to discover. Some of my favorite homeschooling moments have been sharing wonder with my children. Remember, homeschooling is not just a window of learning and discovery for your children; it's right in front of you to enjoy and learn from. Find the wonder!

*Work*

At times, I've wondered if we focused on a good work ethic too much or if we were right to teach character and ownership in our schoolwork and all we put our hands to. Homeschooling families must find their own rhythms and systems to keep their families operational and in unity. An oft forgotten part of homeschooling culture is the value of work, responsibility, and stewardship, not only for the benefit of our children's personal education but for the benefit of the entire family and for their future. Remember, your home is an extension of your homeschool.

I have now seen the fruits of our efforts and the effects of ensuring that the value of work is incorporated into our homeschooling. We can accomplish this by creating focus areas we then assign to our children. This might mean allowing them to be responsible for helping with meals, ministering to other families or neighbors through odd jobs and chores, and learn the importance of reaping and sowing. Teaching them to apply themselves diligently in all things will bear forever fruit, far surpassing what we could ever imagine.

With some of our children on the other side of graduating and watching them navigate their lives, I can see the value of making a good work ethic part of our homeschooling years. They didn't fumble over self-care, job searches, filling out applications, earning an income to pay for their bills, or responsibility for their things and stewardship of their surroundings.

It was in the simple everyday actions of home life and academics that these lessons would unfold. My goal was to raise responsible and hard-working adults. This was part of their education.

*Well Done*

You are raising adults. When you sit down day after day, month after month, and year after year, laying a foundation of learning and love, you are adding to the person they will become. Your investment matters. Homeschooling is about raising a whole person and doing our best to do it well. On hard days when we give a little bit more, on easy days when we go the extra mile to find the wonder, in moments when we want to stop the whole journey, and when we are worried our kids are just not getting it, we keep going, working, praying, and loving *well*.

Modeling and teaching our children perseverance will help develop this trait. We didn't just get our work for the day "done," but we did it with our best effort and pushed through the tough stuff. We do more than "what is required." We don't put in the time because we have to. We show up and work with the best attitude and work ethic we can.

*Homeschooling well means more than average or acceptable.*
*It is giving the best we have.*

*Woven*

You have been given the privilege and job to weave the strongest threads of character, virtue, knowledge, and academia into the fabric of your child's life. The culture of our home can be the golden thread that is stronger and stands out among the rest. Your home is the place that binds their character to truth. Your direction and love will guide them.

You cannot see the end in view yet, but you have hope from knowing the love and the work you are investing into your home now will remain with your children forever. Every area of your home and their schoolwork is a formative part of your children's lives.

*· · · · · · · personal reflection · · · · · · ·*

What is the culture of our home and school? Am I intentional to weave the most important virtues and habits into our homeschooling?

*· · · · · · · personal challenge · · · · · · ·*

Make a list of the virtues, habits, attitudes, foundational principles, and character you think is important for your child to develop before they leave home. Begin by breaking those areas down into small, bite-sized daily practices and add them into your family culture.

*· · · · · · · drawing from the well · · · · · · ·*

Setting our minds on heavenly things is our first discipline and deliberate step to establishing a culture that sets a trajectory worth working for.

> *"Finally, brothers, whatever is true, whatever is honorable, whatever is just, whatever is pure, whatever is lovely, whatever is commendable, if there is any excellence, if there is anything worthy of praise, think about these things."*
> Philippians 4:8

*· · · · a prayer for my homeschool · · · ·*

Lord, help us to desire You to be at the center of all things. May we never lose the wonder You created in all of us. Help our home to be "others" focused. Help us remember to work hard and to not forget You in our home and everyday lives. We praise You for giving us this home and our children, and we ask that You use our home for Your glory and that our children will learn Your precepts and Your way here first. In Jesus' name, Amen.

# chapter 11

# The Wisdom
# to Surrender

*D*oes every family have one child (or maybe two) who says black when you say white? They wear shorts when you suggest pants. You correct their pencil grip every day for two years straight and they still just hold on to it for dear life with a crooked fist. You ask them to line up their math problems in columns and they do all the work in their head . . . and you can't check their work. They read in the dark when you tell them it is bad for their eyes, and you ask them to read out loud with the group and they lag a few seconds behind or ahead of everyone else. Their study area can't be close to anyone else's because noise is distracting to them, but they talk to everyone during lessons, just to have a social connection.

You know this child. There will be days and moments when we need to make hard and fast decisions to choose our battles. Otherwise, we become mom, teacher, principal, corrector, enforcer . . . and the list continues.

I have lost entire hours, and, on a few occasions, entire days of our homeschooling as small battles turned into all out "wars." My reaction and the pressing in of the circumstances completely derailed any teaching, positivity, or attention span from my child(ren), and I became the center of a conflict we could not turn around without a dismantling of the day, until I could pinpoint when everything began to unravel.

There are battles and then there are wars. There is victory and defeat. There are victors and then, those defeated. Your homeschooling journey will be full of hills and valleys, victory and defeat. But you do not have to be "the defeated." At the end of the story, we also don't want to discover we've made ourselves the hero, the one who had to fight every battle or had to suffer through the tough stuff alone when we could have instead chosen our battles wisely and won the war—as a team.

There is no denying there will be problems and conflicts in our home and around our schoolwork. We don't have to throw our hands up or engage in a battle of the wills. There will be your way, their way, and no way on some days. There will be days when you don't think you (or your kids) can do anything right. And there will be days when you are singing praises over your children and celebrating their victories.

## SURRENDERING THE PERFECT HOMESCHOOL

The perfect homeschool is a myth. Surrendering ideals or visions of a completely "normal" day is the most freeing homeschool gift you can give yourself and your children. When we place success on a ladder above relationships, we begin a spiral of imbalance, and the small struggles become bigger over time. Pursuing perfection at the cost of being real will become a war of hearts and minds in the end because no one can live with a façade. Our homeschooling will be as real as life gets by the mere fact that we live in such proximity to one another.

Surrendering perfection may mean choosing to defuse a momentary struggle over proving you may be right. Your conflicts may have to be handled with patience, grace, conversations, and heart-to-heart talks outside of school time. There will be homeschooling moments that expose the imperfections in your home. We all have them. We all live with an undercurrent of relational conflict, but homeschooling brings us face to face with the unexposed or unaddressed things we might normally ignore, be ignorant of, or never have seen as a concern.

Homeschooling means heart work, homework, and healthy work. Letting go of the daily trivial pursuits, perfectly behaved children, and straight As will give us the freedom to not look perfect, but to show up where we are needed the most. Facing the giants is hard work. Give your children a safe space to learn how to handle their conflicts, process their feelings, and ask hard questions. Be attentive even when you disagree and help them navigate challenges. This will require you to surrender your time and your expectations.

You may need to let go of the neat and tidy schedule you created to work one-on-one with your child who is struggling. Your family will need to learn the art and healing of an apology.

Your homeschool may be flipped upside down in the middle of seasons of sickness, trauma, diagnosis, and financial instability. Your surrender of control may be the very thing your home and school need. Your children may need you to tell them you are not perfect, and neither is your homeschooling, but you are and will do your best to be present and to not try to be perfect. Your children may need firmer boundaries, structure, and a controlled or relaxed environment for effective learning and stronger relationships.

Surrendering the perfect homeschool will require wisdom and patience.

## SEEKING WISDOM

The word wisdom is referenced over two hundred times in the Old Testament. I have found value and growth in my parenting and my homeschooling when I seek wisdom from the Word of God and from other wise and veteran homeschoolers. When we face conflict in our homeschooling, we need more than our emotions, our human responses, and our limited resources to draw on to find solutions and navigate this new territory.

Wisdom is gained from asking questions and learning in humility. When we seek His wisdom, we have a strength beyond our own to persevere in our calling to homeschool.

Wisdom gives us the ability to view our challenging days through asking questions, a love of learning, and perspective.

### Asking Questions

Rather than engaging with your child over every little problem and difference you will have, you can wisely allow curiosity to prompt you to ask questions of your child. By doing so, you'll see beneath the surface of the conflict and discover what was propelling their actions and attitudes. Many conflicts in our home could have been avoided if I hadn't reacted and jumped to conclusions. When we're annoyed, our default is to react in a negative way rather than look deeper for answers. When taking the time to ask questions, I usually found my child had good reasons for their choices.

The choice to ask questions isn't to ignore a child's poor choices or unacceptable behavior, but this causes us to slow the pace and make space to work through these moments. Sometimes we don't really care or want to know what is going through our child's mind or their reasons behind poor choices, but asking questions gives everyone time to defuse and act wisely. Asking questions communicates value to others. Remember that asking questions isn't always about communicating the consequences. That comes later. Right now, we are engaging in a productive way.

During conflict, we may not think quickly or clearly, and the ability to come up with sincere questions is often absent. Below are some questions to keep in the back of your mind for the days you need to open doors to new conversations and solutions.

- Is there a reason you didn't do all the math problems on this page?
- Can you tell me why you ignored me when I told you to have your bed made and your water bottle packed before co-op today?
- What were you doing the whole time you told me you were reading, and I was making lunch?
- Would you like me to sit down and do your lesson with you?
- Are you having a hard time understanding today's lessons? Would you like me to explain it again?

- Are you having a hard day? Is there something bothering you that you would like to share?
- Would it help to do this in a different way?
- Can you step away from the school room and spend some time alone in another space until you can communicate clearly with me (us)?

## Love of Learning

Many times, we forget that struggles in our homeschool are often, at the root, character problems; yet we treat them as academic problems. But let's not forget that not every child (or even mama) will love learning. Not everyone is an educator or has a passion for the process of learning new things and spending time together with their parents or siblings doing so.

We can lean into our child's learning styles, learn what excites and motivates them, and change things that bring great struggle, conflict, or discouragement to both them and to ourselves. I didn't know I had this choice or the tools to do this when I was homeschooling my first three children. Three decades of homeschooling and leaning into wisdom and the love of learning has shown me the value of adapting, pivoting, and creating a love of learning that is unique to each child. This takes work and requires creativity. The more we learn about our children, the less the struggle becomes about us. We begin to see a conflict before it happens, preempt stressful moments with questions and react differently.

It takes time to love what we do. It takes discovery, wisdom, and patience. Here are a few questions to ask *yourself* that will help you choose your battles.

1. Does my child communicate their frustrations or struggles to me consistently?
2. Have I identified if my child is upset or frustrated because of learning disabilities?
3. Does my child seem to have a strong will or a defiant character concern?
4. What motivates my child to learn? Do they work well with goals, rewards, checklists, open spaces, or timelines, or do they feel stifled, locked in, stir crazy, need movement and more independence?
5. What have they missed in their learning that leaves them struggling in certain areas of academics? Are there formative elements in certain subjects that were skipped, rushed through, or avoided? Is that missing foundation now causing them frustration and diminishing their love of learning?
6. What excites my child as a person? Do I give them outlets for those things or use them as a consequence when they don't "perform" well academically?
7. Is my child bored or not challenged enough, and what can I do about this?
8. Do I inspire my children to love learning? Do I get excited over simple lessons, new ideas, and showing up to increase in knowledge?
9. Have I created such a serious homeschool space that the love of learning has been squashed?
10. How can I inspire my children to learn their way?

*Perspective*

Wisdom grants us perspective and allows us the ability to see the bigger picture. We're able to better understand the child, their heart, and their academic needs and to see beyond the crisis moments. Wisdom also gives us the long-term perspective. Sometimes, homeschooling conflicts can feel like an "all or nothing" situation and we have a difficult time remembering they are momentary, and the solutions will change the trajectory of any future problems. We want to throw in the towel or put an exclamation mark at the end of "this isn't working!" The wisdom in surrender is not defeat, but holding on to the hope that we made a difference, and it help will determine the future.

Looking back, I can see my lack of wisdom in certain situations or conflicts and wish now I'd had a broader perspective. That would have changed the trajectory of some of our homeschooling outcomes. If there was one thing I could shout from the rooftops about a mother's homeschooling perspective, it would be this:

*Homeschooling is very personal for a mother,*
*but we shouldn't take the conflicts personally.*

Whatever the struggles may be, it is natural for us to think they are about us. Moms feel all the feelings, and we tend to take the struggles or conflicts personally. Our feelings can skew our perspective, and we use words like "ungrateful" and "stressful" with our children to communicate our feelings in the moment. Our children do not have the big picture perspective we have. They do not know the weight you carry in homeschooling them. They are following and trusting your lead in this and do not understand the sacrifice, the work, and how very personal homeschooling is to you.

Every day you wake up and make the whole day about them. You plan lessons and labs and learning stations, and every day they show up trusting your long-term perspective. Their laziness, words, restlessness, inattentiveness, and eruptions are not personal but can still feel that way, and this gets in our way as we attempt to separate their behaviors and our personal feelings. Take the personal out of the struggle and your perspective will shift.

## SURRENDERING THE LABELS

In my earlier years of homeschooling, this chapter would have freed me from the captivity of conflict in my home, but also equipped me as I reconciled the ideal homeschool student, or "normal" child, with the reality of teaching a child with learning or behavioral challenges. So many questions plague homeschooling moms as they hit roadblocks, see red flags, and face daily struggles. Once we surrender the idea that all our children should fit into a mold or label, then we can begin to adopt the unique approach to our home and school instead of working against our children.

Our children feel the pressure and the conflict when we go against the grain to homeschool them differently. They know they are struggling and can obviously see that we are too. When we find peace in accepting that our homeschooling journey will be different, we will thrive and so will our children.

Homeschooling a child with learning struggles, a strong will, attention problems, hyperactivity and sensitivity, and personality clashes can be one of the hardest and loneliest struggles for a homeschooling mom. We tend to isolate ourselves from the community we know we desperately need because we think it will be too hard for a child to adapt and for us to bring the challenges with us. They are always with us.

## SURRENDERING THE WIN

Not every battle has to be won. Often, raising a white flag in humility, showing up with solutions, or walking away is better than always needing to be right. There will always be one more word you could say, one more thing you could do, another consequence you could hand out, or another lost day of lessons because the battle of wills lasted the entire school day. It doesn't have to be that way.

Your wins will look different than normal, surprising you when you least expect it. The challenging writing lessons you helped them work through for days—the creative energy and resources you have put into their environment to help them focus and stay on track and the tears of reading through a whole chapter—those are big victories and worth celebrating. What may take another student half the time and half of your effort is a big win for the mom and student who struggled, persevered, and did it—together! Every word, challenging moment, every tear, prayer, lesson repeated, work done and redone, and endless hours of conflict resolution will someday be worth it!

*Homeschooling wins show up when we least expect them to, reminding us that learning is a process, and the small moments lead to great victories.*

## CELEBRATE THE WINS

Learning to mark the hard-earned victories is the first step to finding peace in knowing your hard work is paying off. We forget to celebrate the small steps that we have been working toward. Take a look at the wins below as you consider your homeschooling challenges. Where can you find a well-earned "well done"?

- When you recognize your reaction time to a potential conflict was delayed and your response was calmer, you could ask questions or direct your child to a place of peace
- When your child has fewer meltdowns or arguments, or you get through one day with a high lesson success rate and a peace in your heart that maybe something is working
- When you see your children stopping their habits before they happen and pivot on their own
- When you know what your child truly needs in the hardest moments and have a solution
- When you realize you are not the yelling mom and teacher anymore
- When your child shows up to their homeschool work with hope and not ready for a battle, discouraged, or apathetic
- When you get to lunch break, and all is calm
- When your children get excited about something in your homeschool day

- When you get excited about something in your home-school day
- When you confidently tell someone else they can home-school
- When you can celebrate the small wins and wait for the bigger victories

## ······· *personal reflection* ·······

Have I taken the challenges in my homeschooling too personally? Have I been able to identify the root of the conflicts and whether they are the result of bad behavior or learning struggles? Have I made an idol out of what an ideal homeschool should look like, and am I part of the conflict I am facing and feeling?

## ······· *personal challenge* ·······

I will begin asking questions before I react. I will remember there is always more to the problem than just academics. I am going to lean into wisdom by reading the Word and learning from other wise homeschooling parents.

## ······· *drawing from the well* ·······

Below I've listed four wise ways we can practice conflict resolution in our homeschool:

1. Attack the problem and not the person.
2. Be honest.
3. Stay current: don't wait to address a concern.
4. Act, don't react.

*"Therefore, having put away falsehood, let each one of you speak the truth with his neighbor, for we are members one of another. Be angry and do not sin; do not let the sun go down on your anger, and give no opportunity to the devil. Let the thief no longer steal, but rather let him labor, doing honest work with his own hands, so that he may have something to share with anyone in need. Let no corrupting talk come out of your mouths, but only such as is good for building up, as fits the occasion, that it may give grace to those who hear. And do not grieve the*

*Holy Spirit of God, by whom you were sealed for the day of redemption. Let all bitterness and wrath and anger and clamor and slander be put away from you, along with all malice. Be kind to one another, tender-hearted, forgiving one another, as God in Christ forgave you."*
Ephesians 4:25–32

···· *a prayer for my homeschool* ····

Lord, help me begin the path of peace in my home and school. I ask for a heart soft toward the heart of my child. Please give me the wisdom and strength to engage when I need to. You are a God of peace and purpose. I am entrusting my homeschooling to You and asking for Your help in modeling positive communication and better habits for us all. Thank You for giving us Your Word and the wisdom we need. In Jesus' name, Amen.

*chapter 12*

- - • • - • • - • • - • • • - - -

# Is This My Job
# or My Identity?

There are a lot of helpful tips and inspiration I can write about in the pages of this book, but this chapter is my "sit down and share over a cup of coffee or tea with you" moment. Let's begin with my story and go from there.

So many years of my homeschooling were spent in a relentless pursuit of achievement—setting goals for academic success; choosing the "right" and sometimes the most expensive curriculum; comparing our progress with the homeschooling families we knew; creating an unachievable schedule; and eating, sleeping, and breathing homeschooling. I bet you are feeling stressed just reading those words. Over time, my physical stamina couldn't keep up with this level of expectation and investment. It wasn't that I wasn't "all in" anymore, but my inability to keep my former pace opened my eyes to an alarming truth. And once this happened, I could see it everywhere and can identify it even today.

*Homeschooling had become my identity.*

Most of our friends were homeschooling, and everything we did was centered around our homeschooling. This is a natural pattern, and there isn't anything wrong with spending time with like-minded friends. But there is a trap with any calling or job in our life, and that is to mix up the roles and confuse one for the other. Homeschooling is often referred to as a calling, and we all know it is a job, and so the lines get muddied. We take our job seriously, devoting our time and efforts to excellence, and investing hours into our children's academic success. Then we add in motherhood and the busy activities life brings and we have moved into a space that we have also made our identity.

I decided to devote a whole chapter to this topic because as a homeschooling mom of almost thirty years, I know this all too well and didn't see the signs in my own life until my youngest three children were in their teens. This sneaky transition happens gradually and is not exclusive to homeschooling moms. I see it in most occupations that require hours of sacrifice. The signs aren't always obvious, yet they're important to talk about. I want to encourage you to read slowly, pray, and ask the Lord for an open heart and mind and introspection where it may be needed in your own life. There are many reasons this chapter should be read and considered in every season of homeschooling and not just during a one-and-done life and identity check. Separating our passionate investment and our identity is difficult because every thought, decision, and plan for our family is centered around our homeschooling. Every day our schedules consist of being the taxi driver, meal maker or planner, teacher, mother, mentor, corrector, and the list goes on.

We have discussed being the hub on the wheel, the center of the motions moving simultaneously. The piece we often lose sight of when we take our role or job seriously is this:

*There is more to life than homeschooling. God may have called you to homeschool your children, but He called you to something bigger and more important first, and that has never changed.*

Finding identity in our homeschooling is not wrong, but if "homeschooling mom" is the only thing we are when our kids have closed their books and the day is done, we are left with an empty space and not knowing who we are and what we were created for. We can live and love homeschooling without it becoming "who we are." We can use our skills and give our time. We can pour our lives into our children, but in the middle of it all, we must take a step back and evaluate who we serve, what we serve, and what has become the "most important thing." This is the crux of the questions we should consider in every season of our homeschooling.

*If you were asked this question,*
*what would your answer be today?*
*"What brings you joy and why do you do it?"*

Whether we are homeschooling or working in a chosen career or ministry, we should ask ourselves how—or in whom—we find our "worthiness" and our "purpose." Otherwise, we are working out all things in the flesh and for our vainglory—and what we sow is what we reap. Our choices aren't always about *what* we are doing, but *who* we are doing it for. Many of us find our identity in the work and value of our homeschooling accomplishments: the success of a project, the achievements of our children, the daily triumph of getting it all done, and the knowledge that you were part of something big, challenging, and important. Yes, these are worth celebrating.

But I have witnessed so many moms completely deflated when a bad day comes along, or their children aren't succeeding. Their emotions, sense of worth, and their investment of time are all tied up in "homeschooling mom." When things don't go as planned, they feel beaten down. When their kids struggle or don't listen, they see their efforts as useless. And when the day is over and the weariness sets in, they don't have much left for anything else, including, at times, their spouses.

When all we hear are the noises of defeat and complaining, we have a hard time hearing or believing the truth and purpose to which we have been called.

## HEARING GOD IN THE WHISPER

I am always moved by the story of Elijah in 1 Kings. I would encourage you to spend time reading through Elijah's story. Elijah's life work was marked with incredible victory and defeat. His hardest moments came on the heels of victory. In 1 Kings 19:11–13, we find Elijah's life in great danger from Queen Jezebel. In fear, he ran for his life and hid from his calling. He began to question what God had called him to do. Even after his previous victories, it was in his lowest moments that Elijah questioned his potential and was ready to give up. Elijah hid on Mount Horeb, dejected and alone. God knew where Elijah was and met Him in his defeat. He called to him in a still small voice, and asked Elijah this question: "What are you doing here, Elijah?"

I am always moved by this passage as I have often felt like Elijah in his weakness, afflictions, and questions. He questions his calling and his identity and has lost sight of his purpose. But God whispers in gentleness to him to get his attention and remind him of the bigger picture. God doesn't harshly scold or demand Elijah to come back to his senses to remind him of his calling and identity.

What if your current discouragement is a sign that you are doing something worthwhile? What if the thing that's missing isn't a new task, but an attitude about your current task?

What if the work you must do isn't just a job, but a calling?

*personal reflection*

Our thoughts dictate our investments:

Do my children's failures define my reactions and my thoughts?

Are most of my concerns, worries, fears, and time centered around homeschooling?

Do I feel like I don't have a life anymore outside of homeschooling?

Do I feel resentment toward homeschooling and the time it takes?

*personal challenge*

Our actions demonstrate the focus of our hearts:

Am I able to step away from homeschooling each day to live out life aside from this work?

What things in my life have I been neglecting because they feel mundane?

What are my thoughts toward others who do not homeschool?

When I consider my life, do I value homeschooling above all else?

Do I hold my homeschooling in higher esteem than others or elevate it above other areas in my life God has called me to?

Where do I spend time outside of homeschooling?

*drawing from the well*

God would not call us and then not equip us. Stepping forward into His promises allows us the freedom to feel unburdened from our heavy weights.

*"Or do you show contempt for the riches of his kindness,
forbearance and patience, not realizing that God's kindness
is intended to lead you to repentance?"*
Romans 2:4 NIV

···· *a prayer for my homeschool* ····

Lord, I know I am called to homeschool my children, but waver when I am weary or compare myself to others. Help me to be rooted in the knowledge that I am Your beloved and you have given me gifts to cultivate that will help bring Your glory to my homeschooling. Help me to remain focused on the calling before me. In Jesus' name, Amen.

# chapter 13

# The Happy in Homeschooling

*M*any homeschool mornings I would turn on a song to wake up our household. I wouldn't blare the music, and I would choose the same song every morning with a little variety thrown in here or there. The songs were generally relaxing, motivating, and cheerful. I would hope that the gentle rise and shine would do its job until I heard feet hit the floor for yet another day of our time together. When I had a semi-decent night's sleep, I would go the extra mile and make pancakes or waffles with a toppings bar, and we would have our breakfast together.

Whether it was slow and cheerful wake up music, special breakfasts for the grumpiness, notes taped to their books or desks, or a midweek change to our schedules, I quickly figured out that homeschoolers need encouragement and the grace of slow starts just like the rest of the world. Not all our mornings were spent in pajamas or reading our favorite books cuddled together on the couch. Not every day was purposeful and unhurried, and not every moment was steady and strong. But over the years, I realized there would be times we remembered how special and foundational they were. The common denominators for all our decisions were intentionality and consistency.

*Homeschooling memories and impact are built on*
*our intentional decisions and our consistent actions.*
*They are vital for a steady pace and to finish with joy.*

## GOLD STAR MOMENTS

At the end of every homeschool day, you will lay your head on your pillow and reflect on behavior, academics, and socialization. Often, we are hard on ourselves and in our evaluations. But there are those gold star opportunities that make our children who they are and who they will become. Let's give ourselves a gold star for the times when we chose to pivot, celebrate, recalibrate, or show up to create an environment of learning. Sometimes we fail to recognize an accomplishment as gold star worthy. When we fail to recognize our strengths, we lose momentum in our resolve and in our pace.

Below are some five star–rated gold star moments from our personal homeschool space that have helped me set a slow and steady pace in areas that can feel hurried and stressful. They allow me to see our growth, bring consistency and flexibility to our schedule, and make our homeschooling spaces happy—because who doesn't want to be happy? After you read through these examples, make a list of the areas you see as potential slow starts or places to pivot in your homeschool to help you all feel less hurried.

*Quiet times every afternoon*

Every afternoon immediately after lunch, all the kids have a quiet reading time in the living room. I began this when they were little and started with small increments of time, then added minutes each year. This reading time wasn't just for me to have uninterrupted or productive catch-up space (although it is super handy for this). Rather, this time unexpectedly helped the kids learn to sit for planned periods of time, quietly and without screens, games, or activities. Their interest in books and reading grew, and they even fell asleep on the days their bodies let them know they needed rest.

I discovered hidden rewards from this daily habit. As I added time incrementally, the children's attention spans also improved when we attended church, plays, or performances. They learned the value of having quiet head space and not always needing to be talking or doing something. They begin to crave consistency and asked for this daily. This quiet time applied to all ages and wasn't to be used for anything other than rest or reading. Every day after lunch cleanup, each child past naptime age and any kiddo who was awake would pick their favorite quiet space, a book, and a blanket, and our home would settle into a peace and quiet mode. As my children grew older, I would often use this time to work with the higher grades and subjects while the littles had reading time, but generally, even the older kids craved this consistency and asked for their reading or rest time.

We had a few rules, and this helped with consistency and avoiding distractions. Below are several guidelines I found to be helpful.

- A timer was always set; there is always a child who is motivated by the timer

- Everyone was within mom's view; we kept this activity centrally located
- No distractions or toys, just books or rest
- No devices or games
- Sometimes we would all listen to an audiobook
- No snacks or getting up and down; minimize movement
- Start the timer with small increments and increase as needed

*Lunch and snack menu choices*

Make a running list of snacks and lunch ideas, and each Sunday evening, post the snack and lunch options for the week. This was a gold star to-do for our homeschool. Often, we feel the need to buy our groceries and then map out every meal. This is great for dinner meal planning until our children are older, but the point of the gold star ideas is to make our days simpler. When you post the week's breakfast, snack, and lunch options based on your grocery hauls, then you have just taken the big decisions, prep, and responsibility off yourself. This may be a new and almost overwhelming concept to you. There is a learning curve to choices and independence for your children and your willingness to surrender control and management of this area, but in the end this process accomplishes the following:

- Allows you more time in the mornings to prepare for the day
- Takes the micromanaging away from you
- Streamlines and manages your grocery list and curbs the overeating of snacks (once it is gone, it is gone)
- Gives your family time to master kitchen skills, independence, and teamwork

- Allows older kids to prepare, plan, and help with younger children
- Makes you the "cool mom" because you seem laid back, think up great ideas, and let them pick

To get started, follow this simple how-to:

1. Choose your breakfast, snack, and lunch ideas for your grocery list
2. Shop for your groceries and organize your pantry areas for those three categories
3. Post your menu for the week on Sunday night
4. Let your kids make their selections for breakfast, snack, and lunch choices based on the list (the groceries are already there)
5. Snacks are based on the list posted; no special requests or complaining
6. Kiddos prep and clean up; helps them consider their choices and time

*First day binder covers*

This activity is a gold star moment that will stay with you and your children for many years to come. There are multiple reasons I have continued this simple yet motivating activity on our very first day of homeschooling each year. It's fun to see their binder cover choices and then, at the end of the year, save them in a portfolio or scrapbook until graduation day. Purchase binders with clear, plastic pocket on the front. The kids can then decorate an 8x10 piece of paper and slide it into the binder pocket.

On the paper they can write their name and draw their favorite summer memory, write a poem, color a picture, write a verse in calligraphy and create a design to go with it, or even take a few days to work on something more complicated that tells a story about who they are or are becoming.

This activity gives them something to look forward to, something to talk about when remembering last year's binder covers, and lightens the serious mood, apprehension, and academic workload of the first day. Sometimes I offer inspirational prompts and ideas to get them started; and as the years go by, they begin considering what they would like their binder to look like ahead of time. I love seeing the different thought processes and products each of my children come up with each year.

*Desk set up*

This is another first day activity and gives your child something special to look forward to. We wipe down our desks, set up our binders, fill pencil cases, and create their special place to learn. When we didn't have desks and did our schoolwork at the table, we would use a crate for storing books and supplies. Giving them a space to organize their things, with a laminated schedule, helped make their first day feel more special than "get out your schoolbooks and let's begin."

*Stickers on folders*

This is my top favorite gold star memory. I cannot even remember how we began this tradition, but it became a big deal in our home and added the consistency these gold star moments accomplish in maintaining a steady rhythm in our home and school. Each of my kiddos would have different colored folders for completed work. After we finished a lesson or a front and back of a worksheet, I would let them choose a sticker from the sticker books we kept in the middle of our school area. I would place a sticker on the page itself, but for more fun, I would put a sticker on the front of their folders also.

The kids watched the front and back of their folders fill up. Their motivation and excitement grew every time they finished a lesson because of the accumulation of these visible and tangible sticker rewards for their hard work. The motivation this propels is remarkable. Try it. I saved their folders for graduation day and included the most creative essays and assignments they'd completed over time.

Homeschooling mamas can forget the importance of visible and tangible rewards for their children's accomplishments. Homeschooling can easily become a checklist because once the work is done, home is for living *after* learning. But this is where we can give ourselves a gold star: instead, we view learning and living as coexisting, and we remember that our children need more than a teacher and a worksheet. They need and crave acknowledgments of their work and efforts. Even if it comes in the shape of a small sticker, it matters.

### Schedule printed and placed in binder

Whether you sit at desks or the kitchen table, whether you do your schoolwork outside, or at a computer, creating a personal schedule for your child will be one of the best ways to raise a responsible child. When creating your child's personal schedule, remember it will help them:

- Stay on task or learn flexibility
- Have a time frame to loosely refer to
- Plan ahead
- Know expectations
- Stay focused
- Practice time management
- Learn their strengths and weaknesses
- Work independently

These schedules will also save you from repeating the next subject.

*Set of goals*

This gold star mom tip will give you a great start and finish to your homeschool journey. Every summer, when I sit down with my personal homeschool notebook, I allot a page for my family, one page per child, and one page for myself. With our big family, that is a lot of pages, but I use my summertime to make lists, ideas, and notes under each name. When I feel like the pages have the content I need, I make a summary of goals per page and person and add these to our actual homeschooling plan for the year.

This is where I say on repeat that home and school are one. If you can see your children through the lens of more than required subjects, this allows you to enhance and build more areas of growth into your homeschooling day, year, and ultimately, their homeschooling career.

Be sure to reserve one of the pages for the family. When you forget you have things to work on as a family unit as part of your home learning, you help develop strong, independent individuals but with little consideration to the team effort and sacrifice required to build one another up. This list making will be vital to creating a strong plan for the year.

Here are the areas you might wish to consider when making lists:

- One list per family member and one for your family
- Strengths: academic, social, physical, enrichment, spiritual, personal
- Weaknesses: don't be afraid to make this list in the same categories as above
- Goals: academic, social, physical, enrichment, spiritual, personal, home, family, friendships, ministry, credits for future plans

Once you have made your lists, break them down into bite-sized pieces and make practical plans and goals per month and add them to your schedule. If you fail to do this step, then everything will stay on your list page and in your heart and head and you will miss the amazing opportunities to mix daily life into your learning each year. Some of your goals will be spread out until graduation and some will be yearly goals. You decide the pace and the space you must add and the practical steps you need to take to reach them.

### Family meetings

This will be a constant support in keeping your pace slow and steady and your schedule on track. Regular family meetings provide opportunities to discuss what is or isn't working in your home, with your schedules, and with behavior and discipline.

*Morning time routines*

A morning routine was a big gold star moment for us daily. There was no rushing to individual assignments, timers were not set for math worksheets or chores, and the pressure of performance was replaced with a love of learning because it was always something new for us all. Every morning, we learned a few new things together to start our day, and it always amazed me that those were the things the children would remember the most.

Just as the world was waking up to the workday, I was reading a Bible story to waking teens, toddlers hanging upside down off the couch, and a baby in my arms. My favorite memories were watching my children retain the stories, choose their favorite poem, and help one another read out loud. They never complained about meeting together in the living room every morning. As the teens got older, I enjoyed getting creative with our morning time. I didn't want them to feel like they were too old for the lessons, stories, and worship, and so I pivoted the teaching from me to them.

Once a week, an older child would read our stories, lead our song time, and cover our character lessons. Their creativity soared as they learned to teach younger children. They adapted lessons to be fun and interactive. I will never forget the faces of our little children listening attentively to their older siblings as they read or acted out a story for all of us. There were no appearances of grandeur or pride. Everyone learned something. I always rotated what we covered in our morning routines to keep them eagerly waiting for what new and exciting thing we would begin our day with.

Those times, the facts, and the learning in the morning together were the things they would share with my husband when he got home or with a grandparent when they asked how homeschooling was going. Our morning times were my gold star moments. The moments when I stood up from the couch after fifteen to twenty minutes of sharing, listening, and learning with my children and knew we did a good thing with our time. I was able to enter the school world for that day with assurance and confidence.

Here are some items we incorporate into our morning time:

- Poetry: fun, simple, whimsical, seasonal, classic, and famous
- Historical figures: basic biographies or facts
- Character qualities
- Bible memory work
- Praise and worship
- Literature: ongoing reading of brief sections of well-loved books

Gold star moments are for us as much as they are for our children. Every home has spaces we create for beauty, rest, play, activity, and learning. Finding rhythms and spaces that we can move our homeschool hours into will help us reset and remind us to keep things light. Discovering and celebrating steady rhythms that bring life to your homeschool will give you and your children the energy to keep going.

###### ······· *personal reflection* ·······

Perhaps I have taken my homeschooling so seriously I have forgotten the reason we are doing this together.

###### ······· *personal challenge* ·······

Make a list of areas you see as potential slow starts or places to pivot to make changes to help your homeschool life feel unhurried. Prioritize adding scheduled routines into your week and remind yourself that those are gold star moments for you too. These will be the most precious times to savor the sweetness of your family time and to watch your children's love for learning grow.

###### ······· *drawing from the well* ·······

This isn't a race won by time, but by learning. Get creative and make sure you reap the benefits homeschooling has for you as well as your children.

*"Do you not know that in a race all the runners run, but only one receives the prize? So run that you may obtain it. Every athlete exercises self-control in all things. They do it to receive a perishable wreath, but we an imperishable. So I do not run aimlessly; I do not box as one beating the air. But I discipline my body and keep it under control, lest after preaching to others I myself should be disqualified."*
1 Corinthians 9:24–27

###### ···· *a prayer for my homeschool* ····

Father God, help me relax and bring joy to our homeschool. I need motivation and inspiration because I am tired, and right now, homeschooling feels hard. Help me run the race with perseverance and strength. In Jesus' name, Amen.

# chapter 14

# The Pressure of Success

*W*e are going to homeschool our children."
There was a long pause and apparent confusion on the faces of the people we were talking to.

"Have you ever heard of homeschooling?"

Blank stare, furrowed eyebrows, and then I could tell the thought was beginning to catch up with their voices. "You mean, you are going to do more work with them after school?"

"No. Our children will stay home for school."

"What? No one does that. Are you serious?"

"Yes."

"That's interesting."

Apparently more than interesting.

"What will they do for friends, grades, and who will teach them?"

"We have all of that covered."

Uncomfortable silence. "We aren't sure we agree with this. How will they go to college or get a job?"

Downward spiral . . .

This is how the conversation went for about ten years. By the end of this time, the first three children in our "homeschooling experiment" were in their early teens and excelling in their social circles, academic studies, and obviously thriving in school and in life. The pressure to succeed at homeschooling was real. I was being watched, graded, judged, and not supported. Sadly, I felt as if I needed to prove the success of homeschooling and prove myself to the onlookers and skeptics. Three decades ago, there were a lot of vocal observers. Today, homeschooling is more widely established, generally "accepted," and yet, the need for homeschoolers to prove their success or achievement still exists. Whether we are conscious of this or not, whether we are working to meet an unseen standard, the world expects results. We can shrug this off, do our thing, do it well, and not think twice about what others may say or do, but in the end, sometimes that outward pressure exists. And because we have set the bar for ourselves and our homeschool high, we feel the pressure.

As with any goals we have set before us, it is helpful to ask ourselves for whom we are working and at what cost. We should evaluate our motivation and how the level of success in our homeschool has affected our family.

When we began homeschooling, it was new and we were in full throttle planning mode; we were inspired, creating, teaching, and motivated by the movement and the privilege to homeschool our children. As time wears on in the homeschooling journey, we either relax and let go, or raise the bar and realize others are or have been watching, and we then put external pressures on our homeschooling and internal pressures on ourselves.

## HERO OF OUR STORIES

The tears just wouldn't stop. My husband felt helpless and did what he has learned to do best when I get to a place where I cannot pinpoint exactly what is wrong or why I am so heavily burdened. He asks me questions that help narrow down the problem and quiet the tears. It didn't take long for us to get to the root of this emotional overflow. I was doing way too much in my home and in my homeschool and trying to maneuver every outcome for every child, subject, household chore, grade, success, and failure.

After homeschooling for many years, I had "created" a well-oiled machine. I was homeschooling our ten children in all their subjects, our schedules were tidy, and the chores were getting done. In fact, we were "getting it all done." Except, all the success came at a cost. I had taken it upon myself to be sure we fit everything in, and the kids were the "well-rounded" homeschoolers everyone expected them to be.

I had made myself the hero of the story. I didn't have family who would or could help. I didn't have a strong homeschool community for years, and I was so busy, I had little room for relationships, rest, or retreat outside of our school days. My kids didn't need a fallen hero. They needed a community, other mentors, fellow homeschoolers, and tutors for subjects I was spending hours studying so I could teach them. I was running myself ragged. My children needed more, and I needed less. So, we pivoted, and I delegated, started a homeschool community, outsourced, stopped thinking about success and more about the people they would become—and our world shifted. My children became self-learners for a few of their subjects, and I taught them how to be independent workers, owners of their schedules, and stewards of their time. They learned how to be a better version of well-adjusted homeschoolers, lead with confidence, and delegate like their mama should have for so many years. I hung up my home-schooling cape and became the best mom and teacher I could be. Everything else was delegated out or creatively filled by someone or something else that wasn't me. My kids loved me more for this! New life was breathed into our homeschool, and those watching from the sidelines had something new to see.

## OTHER CHARACTERS IN OUR STORIES

There will always be a crowd on the sidelines of homeschooling circles. I have given them a name: the Spectators. They watch from afar (or maybe sometimes too close) and don't really say anything to us directly, although their opinions are clearly heard by their lack of support. They may be "silent," but we feel the disapproving looks, their lack of enthusiasm when we share homeschooling up-dates, or the periodic check-ins to see how everything is "really" going. This is my favorite crowd because I think homeschoolers are just their spectator sport and they don't have anything in-vested in the game, but they do have the "you do you" mindset. They aren't intrusive and may seem judgmental, but it doesn't weigh on you like those who are closest to you.

Then there are the Intruders. Those who are Spectators but also feel the need to get involved where not invited, share un-solicited and critical advice, and question your every decision. They show little respect to the time needed to homeschool and remind you that public school is always an option. In contrast, the Encouragers will stay with you for the long haul, whether they completely agree or may be skeptical (for a while). They are and will remain your people. Yes, they are watching and waiting in the wings if you need them, but after your diligence, time, and homeschooling bears fruit, they become your favorite people. They are involved and supportive. They are your cheerleaders on the sidelines. The Encouragers will give advice when needed, lend a helping hand, give you the boost you need to succeed long-term by helping you meet short-term goals, listen without judgment, and come alongside your kids to encourage them to the end.

*Homeschooling success isn't defined by grades and a career,*
*but the measure and means by which you get to the end.*
*Be careful of the voices and influences you allow to define*
*the worth of your hard work.*

## WHAT HAS YOU DISTRACTED?

One of the biggest and most unseen obstacles to homeschool success is distraction. There are, and always will be, one more thing to do, areas left undone, or activities that appear shinier, more exciting, or more appealing but that pull us away from our homeschooling focus. We should always be on guard for the things we are most likely to be drawn to. Our passions and pursuits don't have to be completely pushed out of our lives, but as with any good thing, balance is the goal. If we know the areas, and even the times of day, where we will feel the most inclined to be pulled away physically or mentally, we would be wise to set up safeguards and parameters. This is how distractions work. They slowly pull us away in small increments of time or through seemly minor decisions, and then, before we realize it, we are moving in the opposite direction of our goal: homeschooling for the win.

Whether it's a phone call, the lure of social media, or a household project, there are many areas we cannot push aside completely. Some, like a household project, we will integrate into our homeschooling schedule. But to step into the rabbit hole of your greatest distraction can lead to a lot of lost time, unfocused children, missing foundational lessons, and an overall distracted approach to your homeschooling. We all understand the importance of balance, and to choose homeschooling first is one of your best tools for success.

## WHO IS IN CONTROL TODAY?

In addition to our daily one thing question, it is equally vital to remind ourselves daily of *who* is in control—our God and sustainer. To forget this means that most of our pursuits will be lost on questioning our own strength and skills and seeing our time as fruitless or meaningless. We were reminded of the slow and powerful grip distractions can have on homeschooling, but let's not ignore the real underlying feelings of discouragement. The best source of assurance, comfort, and strength to disband discouragement is the knowledge that God is in control, and He is the real proponent of our success in this journey.

Homeschooling with Jesus at the center is our best motivator for success. He is not only a Spectator, a Cheerleader, the Encourager, but He our sovereign Lord and our Comforter who ministers to us when we feel like we can't hold it all together anymore. Any pursuits or purposes we attempt to carry out on our own or in our strength and wisdom apart from God will be a failure; any success will be fleeting, temporary, and empty. We cannot leave Jesus, God, and the Holy Spirit out of our homeschooling and expect to finish well. When we forget about Him in this big thing, we make little time for Him in the small things.

Homeschooling is big and so is our God. He will be with you when you lie down at the end of a long day and need to be reminded you are not failing your kids. He will convict you and show you wisdom when you are distracted or need to change. God is the One we commit our ways to when we wake up every day. When we foolishly think we have a good thing going and we are the heroes because of our own efforts, our definition of success is flawed and will not stand up. He doesn't call us to homeschooling to succeed on our own. A strong homeschooler has committed her ways and her family to the Lord by listening to His leading and surrendering control to Him. Jesus calls us to persevere, but also gives us wisdom. Wisdom listens and leads but does not run the race alone.

One of the best tools to alleviate the pressures we feel as homeschoolers is to learn the goal setting and tracking habit of "choosing one thing." You can make this a daily goal and habit, or a weekly or monthly success tracker for you and your homeschooling. Often, we lose ourselves, our schedules, and the ability to grade or track exactly how well everyone is doing, until we sit down at the end of a long week or the end of the year.

*"Come to me, all who labor and are heavy laden, and I will give you rest. Take my yoke upon you and learn from me, for I am gentle and lowly in heart, and you will find rest for your souls."*
Matthew 11:28–29

Staying the course in your homeschool journey may be the hardest work you will ever do because you are doing important work. The course of your homeschooling career will present you with many choices. The long haul of this journey is going to make you a better parent, a lifelong learner, a student of your child, a jack-of-all-trades, a specialist, a seasoned and veteran counselor, and most importantly, a dedicated mom to your children. It will also make you reliant on your Father—the Who at the center of your homeschooling and your life.

········ *personal reflection* ········

Are there tasks in my home and school that I do not need to be doing? What have I taken on and feel overwhelmed with that someone else can do?

········ *personal challenge* ········

Today, I give God the glory for all *He* has done in and through my children's lives and learning. I turn control back over to Him and will allow my children to see an example of surrender and balanced servant leadership.

········ *drawing from the well* ········

Take your prayers and petitions to God, thanking Him for the work set before you. Allow His peace to transform your homeschool.

*"Do not be anxious about anything, but in every situation,*
*by prayer and petition, with thanksgiving, present your requests*
*to God. And the peace of God, which transcends all understanding,*
*will guard your hearts and your minds in Christ Jesus."*
Philippians 4:6–7 NIV

····· *a prayer for my homeschool* ·····

Dear Lord, I want the best for my children, and sometimes I think my own doubt or my unrealistic expectations of success are the very hindrance to our homeschooling well. Help me in my unbelief and renew in me a steadfast hope in Your control and wisdom in our homeschool. In Jesus' name, Amen.

# part three

# Finish with Joy

"Fear arises when we imagine everything depends on us."[3]

**ELISABETH ELLIOT**

3. Elisabeth Elliot, *The Music of His Promises: Listening to God with Love, Trust, and Obedience* (Grand Rapids: Revell, 2000), 63.

# chapter 15

# Cultivate Curiosity, Creativity, Personalities, and Passions

We have a running joke in our home now that half of our children are graduated and have families of their own, and I am wrapping up my homeschool career with my last three. The younger version of myself homeschooled very differently than I do now. I was "all in" with activities and outlets and always searching for anything and everything we could to make homeschooling the best experience for everyone. I chased fun, created opportunities, and pursued the best fit for the ten personalities and passions everyone under one roof needed. It was exhausting, fun work.

But the standing joke is that my children, young and old, do not remember me in that way. They don't remember me getting down on the floor to teach them new games or chasing them on the playground, pushing them on the swings, taking hikes in the woods to collect leaves or explore new trails to identify trees. I now joke that I have never been good at being the "fun mom" because they define fun differently now. I proudly gave myself the title of "Fun Maker" and am okay with this. The more children I had, the more fun they had living life together, while I was busy making memories with the littles, cultivating the ideas for them to put into action, and creating a homeschool environment where learning is every day and not just a high and low of activities or big momentous occasions.

Cultivating curiosity and creativity is still my favorite part of homeschooling. If we don't foster thinking, new ideas, discovery, and creative learning, how will our children ever learn to think outside the box, see their way around problems, or have a desire to discover something on their own? Although I have recently observed a new wave of homeschooling ideas focused primarily on letting kids be kids and giving them free range to discover and be curious on their own, I also have learned this is a part of your daily homeschooling and not just a free time and discovery phase. Not all children are wired to learn and have independent curiosity, even when given the opportunity. There are some skills that are even more helpful, when parents provided and guided, that help foster this in our children. Remember they are individuals and there is a not a one-size-fits-all formula for their learning styles. This is where the rubber meets the road in learning, where we dig deeper into the wells of learning, celebrate who our children are and who they are going to be, and help them pursue their passions.

My children may not remember me as the most engaged or fun mom, but their lives are living examples of chasing and cultivating their curiosity, passions, and personalities, and that means more to me than fame. I want to be famous for celebrating their growth, not gaining glory for their God-given gifts.

Let's unpack what it looks like to cultivate discovery and adventure in our homeschool. Every day is an opportunity to discover your children's passions and unique personalities. Take a few moments in each section below, as you evaluate and consider each area in your own homeschool. The joy of celebrating curiosity and creativity gives your homeschool life. Finding passions and pursuits to pair with your child's personalities will bring joy to their homeschool journey.

In our gospel-oriented homeschooling, we are drawn to how our Creator's amazing details connect to our everyday lives. We can show our children His attention to details and direct their minds to a curious desire to learn and study more. We want our children to consider His handiwork. I've shared a few verses we have memorized in our morning time together. The Psalms are full of praise for the majesty of God and celebrating His splendor and creation. It is my goal to always refocus our learning onto the truth of God's Word, so my children will remember where His truth can always point us back to His glory.

The following verses from the book of Psalms have been good reminders to me to bring our questions back to His creation and purpose. I am encouraged to point my children to God as we learn about and study what He has created for us to enjoy, which brings Him glory.

"I will consider all your works and meditate on all your mighty deeds." (Ps. 77:12 NIV)

"One generation commends your works to another; they tell of your mighty acts. They speak of the glorious splendor of your majesty—and I will meditate on your wonderful works. They tell of the power of your awesome works—and I will proclaim your great deeds." (Ps. 145:4–6 NIV)

"Come and see what God has done, his awesome deeds for mankind!" (Ps. 66:5 NIV)

Now we will look at four areas in which you can create a culture of discovery in your homeschool. As you read, think about how these may apply in your homeschool.

*Cultivate Curiosity*

Whether we are reading together, walking in the woods, listening to audiobooks, spending time in the Word, attending an event, visiting a museum, or engaged in play dates or a science experiment, I always pause and ask my children questions. This is my trademark even today. I have become so used to sparking discussions, I don't even recognize how often or how many questions I ask in a homeschool day. Asking questions turns a child's brain into action mode. The first step to being curious is independent thinking. Once I have asked my children a question, I am intrigued to hear all the different responses. Usually, they are never the same. With all of our art history studies, I would read a mini biography of the artist as they studied the art example in front of them.

As I circled around the school table and asked what they observed in the artwork, each child had a different and unique perspective. Some of the kids didn't see the art for the color and design, but noticed the emotions represented. Some were drawn to lines and details. By studying artists' lives and their work, my children not only recognized these pieces visually, but they had a connection to each piece. I love this part of cultivating curiosity. I get the privilege of seeing, hearing, and understanding the unique design and delight our Creator has in each of our children. I grow in intrigue and amazement as I watch their minds unfold the wonders, questions, and discoveries before them. My children have learned to pause and think when I ask questions. They don't see those moments as annoying interruptions but welcomed conversations.

*Asking questions nurtures curiosity that leads to conversation.*

I won't always have an answer when they ask questions with (or out of) curiosity. In fact, I don't feel bad if I don't. That is the gift of wonder. It takes us to the next step of discovery. Children learn and retain information and ideas when they do the work, and they ask the questions. We are conversation starters and idea generators and do not need to bear the burden of all-knowing. Not all children think the same way and will not be excited or have the same interests, and that is more than okay.

God has made them uniquely, and it is a beautiful thing to see what they become curious about, as well as how we can encourage them to discover ideas and areas outside of their initial leanings or interests. Our children do not know all the Creator has to offer unless we share it with them. What may seem like a foreign and uninteresting concept may turn out to be the one thing God created them to be amazing at. We won't know unless we train our children to be curious.

Below are questions to ask your children that will help build curiosity:

Have you ever heard of that?
Would you like to learn more about this?
What can we learn from this new idea?
Would you like to try doing this?
Is there something about this that confuses you?
How many things about this can we learn?
What is the purpose?
How did that happen?
Why did it do that?
What makes this work?
Can you make this yourself?

Curiosity is not only sparked by conversations, but also by opportunities. I took it as a challenge to find new concepts, ideas, experiments, nature, books, and current events and place them before my children's eyes and minds. I would have an arsenal of ideas in my homeschool toolbox or be inspired by something we were reading or concepts I knew they needed to learn for that year.

*Not every lesson won is found on the page of a book.*

From fall days by the lake on a blanket with watercolors, a picnic lunch, each child facing a different direction, with a different perspective and capturing what their eyes only could see to a local hands-on field trip, camera packed, notebooks, crayons, and a paper bag to collect nature's souvenirs—the creativity can be spontaneous or planned. By giving your children simple tools and ideas, you are cultivating a sense of discovery.

## Spark and Encourage Creativity

When I chat with other homeschool moms, they tell me that one of the most gratifying and exciting experiences is being part of their child's learning process and witnessing those "lightbulb moments." Those moments are a gift to us. As our children get a little older, the moments are not as monumental because the formative lessons have been established.

The outlets of their creative interests could be endless; therefore, it is important we do not feel burdened to the process of exposure to new and constant ideas all of the time. Consider your child's age, season of life, availability, schedule, and your finances and capacity before signing your child up for every enrichment hobby and elective. There is nothing like exhaustion to snuff out the torch of inquiry. Kids become weary of chasing ideas and crave a home base when they lose their foundational time at home. Choosing the right focus areas and the right time to explore will settle your homeschool into balanced spaces.

We have the amazing gifts of time, resources, and ingenuity to present opportunities for curious learning to our children every day. When we teach a science lesson, we have 101 ideas for presenting the content of the subjects. From asking questions, to setting up science stations in our home, to research and hands-on exploration, we will witness our children wake up to God's creation around them. Be spontaneous and skip the redundant reading of every sentence in their textbooks. When the sunshine beckons you, put the spelling test aside until after dinner and collect rocks, press leaves, or jump rope together. Bring science, history, literature, music, art, and the Bible to life in your home.

Take your children into the woods with their tree identification pocket manual or to the lake or park with a sketchbook. Search for milkweed and caterpillars and take them home to watch the beautiful God-made process of metamorphosis as it transforms into a monarch butterfly. Listen to audiobooks together. Make raised landforms with papier mâché, learn new instruments, use online art lessons for free, and paint famous artists' work each month. Set up sensory bins by color and theme with food and culture discussions. Let your learning be dictated by their lessons and their curiosity. Find a way to teach your children outside the box. Think of their textbooks as a guide for content to be covered, and then don't be afraid to stray far beyond the margins of those books. Homeschooling your children means learning is led by the fine print, those areas your children are curious about.

*You don't need permission to study any idea or topic you would like at any time. Textbooks are just a guide to keep us on track. Make a list of ideas, concepts, or skills you would like your children to learn and make them part of your everyday homeschool.*

A gospel-centered homeschool cultivates a theology and thought process that brings all curiosity back to God and His Word. While asking questions, we also have answers for the knowledge our children are still growing in. As you gradually expose your child to new and exciting ideas and opportunities, remember the purpose is not merely entertainment or to defeat boredom, although those are the perks of discovery. With every pursuit, a gospel focus is going to also grow your child's view of God and their faith in our Creator. They will learn to see life through a lens of faith, and their worldview will grow under your discovery together, always pointing back to Jesus. Their questions will begin to take on the form of answers. Their curiosity will lead to a greater discovery and the bigger picture of God's creation and our purpose. The world is an open book of discovery, and we can use those moments to point to God in all we see and experience.

This has been a literal homeschooling life verse for me over the last thirty years of raising my children:

> *These words I command you today shall be on your heart. You shall teach them diligently to your children, and shall talk of them when you sit in your house, and when you walk by the way, and when you lie down, and when you rise. You shall bind them as a sign on your hand, and they shall be as frontlets between your eyes.* (Deut. 6:6–8)

## Personalities

Homeschooling ten children has reminded me over and over that not only do children have different learning styles, but their personalities are just as important to their learning. If I had tried teaching the same lessons the same way to ten different children, we would have raised robots who could regurgitate information and data. This was not my goal when we chose to homeschool. The struggle in the beginning was that no one told us our children's personalities would be such an integral part of our home-schooling. It required me to teach them on many different levels and to discover who God made them to be. We are all always a work in progress, and as homeschooling moms, we are working with God's precious design and stewarding the growth and molding of who our children become. We can never mess up badly enough that God's plan and purpose for our children would be thwarted.

Learning how our children think and giving them the opportunities to strengthen and grow their curious faith is our primary goal. Every child has unique gifts and callings that will dictate the outlets they lean into. Our amazing job is to be in tune with those and to steward them well. Pay attention to details, little hints of natural talents, personality strengths, and even parts of their "personhood," which may need to be fostered and grown to step into the place of purpose in which God has called them to.

*Our children are not born with a sign that tells us, "I was born for*
*_____, so teach me_____." If it were that easy, then*
*anyone could teach our children. But we are the ones showing up,*
*mining for the gold deep within and on the surface, to sift and*
*polish as plants grown up and pillars of faith for their future.*
*This is homeschooling.*

*Passions*

By the age of eight, most of my children showed particular interests in specific areas I noticed they enjoyed pursuing or had a curiosity about. I paid close attention to the questions they asked or the way they chose to spend their free time. I noticed patterns, likes, and dislikes.

My oldest son loved music. He sang, hummed, and enjoyed listening to music in his free time. He was a quick learner, never liked to be sitting still, and didn't like tedious, slow work. We decided to begin piano lessons for him at the age of four. He caught on quickly and progressed to performing competitively. Today, he is a worship leader. One of our daughters loved to write letters to missionaries in many different countries. She was a strong writer with great penmanship and a curiosity about the world. She hung a large wall map in her bedroom and used push pins to mark the locations of the missionaries with whom she corresponded. She studied the countries and their cultures and learned various languages through her self-study. Her Christmas lists included online language lessons and travel books. While getting her college degree, she volunteered to be an English tutor, and she now travels the world as a hobby when she has time off from her job in communications. Our firstborn daughter carried her camera everywhere as a kid. Every field trip, event, and vacation were recorded by her. For Christmas, she received camera gear, and rather than choosing college first, she trained and apprenticed with a professional photographer. She went on to have her own professional photography business.

We homeschool toward our children's God-given passions their personalities were created for. Their passions can lead to their pursuits. We can put opportunities before our children to train, direct, and prepare them to walk in the purpose God created them for. As we homeschool into the middle and later years, we transfer our energies and time from exposing our children to many different opportunities to a narrower field of choices that focuses on their strengths and cultivates their creativity. Often it is like mining for gold to find the places that bring them joy and to grow their talents.

You will become your child's guidance counselor. Your eye will be trained to see their gifts. Your heart will be in tune to the obstacles and the fear rising that keeps them from trying new things. Your hands and feet will work hard to give them new opportunities and your mouth will speak truth into their lives and future when needed. You will become more attentive to details, while setting goals for the future. You will learn to enjoy the daily moments in your homeschool, knowing the impact every day will have on your future.

*Homeschooling in the final stretch means seeing the whole picture, the whole child, and partnering with God to steward them to His plan and purpose for their lives.*

To know *how* to cultivate and grow their natural passions and interests, we must learn how to see what is before us. God created each of our children uniquely. Once you learn to see their strengths, the struggle to know how to lead them seems so much less daunting.

Below are some tips on how to see and seize opportunities to "mine for gold."

*Mining for "Gold"*

- See their struggles as areas of potential growth, academically and spiritually.
- Remind them that fears and failures are opportunities for us to let God have control and help us.
- Find the spaces and places that make them curious, intrigue them, or bring them joy.
- Focus on their natural strengths with extra lessons, more work, and training.
- Eliminate chasing extra hobbies for the sake of being busy.
- Use time wisely and research areas to pair with strengths.
- Do hard and uncomfortable things.
- Learn, study, and try new things to help narrow their focus.
- Ask questions.
- Interweave discussions about faith and God's will into their life plan and choices.
- Spend time in the details, teaching them to work with excellence.
- Teach them a good work ethic and Christ-centered moral compass.
- Help them make confident decisions.
- Get them involved in ministry, using their passions and pursuits for the Lord.

*········ personal reflection ········*

I know so much more about my children from asking questions and allowing them to ask them of me. I am moved to use those opportunities to point them back to Jesus, the author and finisher of their faith.

*········ personal challenge ········*

I will begin to cultivate my child's passions and work with their unique personality and not against it when it is inconvenient or difficult.

*········ drawing from the well ········*

I have found the greatest delight in mining for the gold of my child's passions. Homeschooling has given me the opportunity to disciple my children. Matching curriculum, enrichment classes, mentors; teaching what God says about their lives and how to steward their time, resources, money, and bodies well; and creating a path to pair with their passions becomes our homeschool role as moms. Our children learn more about themselves and their faith than any book or lesson could cover.

> *"May our sons in their youth be like plants full grown, our daughters like corner pillars cut for the structure of a palace; may our granaries be full, providing all kinds of produce; may our sheep bring forth thousands and ten thousands in our fields; may our cattle be heavy with young, suffering no mishap or failure in bearing; may there be no cry of distress in our streets! Blessed are the people to whom such blessings fall! Blessed are the people whose God is the LORD!"*
> Psalm 144:12–15

*···· a prayer for my homeschool ····*

Lord, You have given me a child intricately created in Your image. As I come before You today, I feel the weight and the immense gift and privilege it is to homeschool and to help mold their personalities and passions into the purpose You created them for. I am asking for wisdom and for a passion that matches this job. Help me to listen well and to point my child back to You in all we do. In Jesus' name, Amen.

*chapter 16*

- - • - •• •• •• • ••• •••

# Making the Grade

*W*e learned by now not to get caught up in others' expectations of us or our children when it comes to homeschooling. To finish well, it is also imperative for us to realize there will be a level of adaptability, accountability, and acknowledgment from a source other than ourselves that will determine our child's future. Across the board, we all know our child will need to make an income, live in the real world, and be equipped with a skill set, training, or higher education once they leave our homeschool.

From the early years, the goal of raising successful kids is always looming in our mind. Along the way, we learn to surrender the fear of the future and transfer it into faith and formation. Time gives us perspective. By now, we know what motivates them, inspires them, how they work, and what they struggle to do or not do. We have an idea of their potential for further education and support they may need. Our ears and eyes have been tuned into opportunities and ideas for their future and now is the time to begin the slow steps to prepare them for the direction they may choose to take

Yes, their academic grades matter as they give us those celebrated mile markers of their potential, bookwork capabilities, and attention span. Their tests and assignments have now shown us if furthering their education is a good fit for them or how we can help prepare them for a trade or a career that doesn't involve college. Be assured you know your child the best and your evaluations of their potential should match your goals and the path you set for them in the final years. Evaluating your homeschooling regularly is beneficial for you, but also to ensure your child is "making the grade." Whether this is meeting state requirements academically and applying themselves where they need to, learning adult life skills or preparing for the future, this is a steady process that requires intentionality.

Our kids will have exciting goals and celebrations as they near graduation. As much as we love seeing our children achieve all those things, we should remember homeschooling can be this but so much more. Making the grade for your child may look entirely different and the pressure of a defined level of success isn't for everyone. The beauty and blessing of homeschooling are raising and teaching individuals without a mass production mindset, where all the pieces unique to that child are taken into consideration as they grow into adults. There will be many decisions ahead of you to decide the direction and achievement your child can and should pursue. I am telling you this now because the pressure we experience in the later years of homeschooling can feel heavy. It reminds me of a receiver holding the football tight, and running fast and furious, eyes set on the goal line; and with every step, he must choose a direction to twist, turn, and pivot, all while keeping the end with the ball tightly secured. You may think you are the receiver, and your child is the football. Rather, your child is the receiver and is feeling a great weight of responsibility and pressured decision-making to reach the end goal, and you are coaching them from the sidelines and from every direction.

Our children feel the significance of those last years, even when apathy seems to be at its peak. At this point in our homeschooling, or any educational path a student is on, these final years are like pulling a tug-of-war rope with you on one end and your child on the other end. Except this pull will require more determination and encouragement from you than ever before. I want you to know this is normal. Everyone is tired and knows the road ahead will mean change. Crossing the finish line will reap a great reward. Some kids just want to finish and never make one more decision again. Others seem to have clarity and strong decision-making abilities and they forge ahead with ease. And then there are those who are weary of the whole discussion and just want the goal setting and conversations to stop for a while. We get to be the cheerleaders and recognize where our children are in each stage of homeschooling. There will be days you will feel like you are pulling them along, and other days they are in sync with the journey, and you feel a weight has lifted. Every child is different, and it is helpful for us to be aware of the differences in our children and to know what to expect.

Know what motivates your child for their future other than pressure and guilt. Some children are self-motivated, while others do not respect schedules or goals. I call these the Motivators and the Dawdlers. Or you may be raising the Doubter, who cannot make a decision because they doubt their own abilities. The Entrepreneurs will keep you on your toes, turning every assignment into a new and exciting idea or opportunity. They keep homeschooling fun and challenging. The Entrepreneurs can be motivating, yet exhausting. And then, we have our Late Bloomers. The "not in a hurry," to grow up or be in a hurry to do just about anything or everything. Give those kiddos the time and space they need. Knowing how our kids are motivated and how they learn will help us help them.

## THE MOTIVATORS

Known for their goal setting, thoroughness, decisiveness, and follow-through, the Motivators are the students you can set up for success (or they will do it on their own). You watch them soar, stumble, get back up, and make new goals, knowing and trusting the process. Motivators are independently motivated and in turn, motivate their peers and siblings to meet similar goals. Some of us are fortunate to homeschool a child like this because we are also motivated to finish strong for them in turn. They may not always be the most confident, but they know anything worth working for is worth the work. This student will need the most support in the last years of homeschooling to keep their eyes on the goal and have a clear and definitive picture, timeline, outline, and tools, and they will be onboard most of the way.

They will struggle when something changes or siderails their original plan but can easily be set back on the right track when they know this is where and what they should be doing. Early on, they will need your reassurance that you see their gifts, they are capable, and this is the right track. Motivated homeschooling students are usually defined by independent learning.

Homeschooling Motivators is rewarding and challenging at the same time. They need encouragement from us, and we must make sure we are meeting this need to keep them on point. Consider giving them the opportunity to work alongside other people and in situations that allow them to learn how to flex under pressure. Usually, Motivators have many abilities and interests and can get caught up in the decision versus the action. Action is their greatest strength, so identifying their God-given gifts and interests early on is your job and privilege as a homeschool mama. Knowing when to press and when to let go and teaching them the difference between good and bad motivators is a life lesson these children will keep with them forever, regardless of what they "do" with their homeschooling.

Here are a few ways to empower Motivators to make the grade:

- Schedule subjects and assignments out to make their time more manageable and not overwhelming.
- Once given the tools for self-taught learning, they can apply the same discovery process in other areas of academics and life.
- Clearly define the timeline along the way for final school years, and in the month leading up to the next steps.
- Discuss academic and any future options, visit, and research possible choices and align with others who have similar goals; this could be college, a trade, or job opportunities.
- Help them identify weaknesses that could potentially derail the goal; independent students learn to work with their strengths to succeed, but weaknesses may be missed because of their independence. Pay attention to notice and help them.

Motivators will often be driven by task-oriented goals and activity. Their relationships, faith, and focus will sometimes take second place to their goals. They often become primarily focused on what is before them and they lose touch with the real-life intentional work it takes to maintain friendships and family unity. Sometimes, these kids work as an "all or nothing" focus to the point of forgetting other areas of life that are just as beneficial. As a homeschooling mom, you have the unparalleled privilege to teach and model how faith and family are the strongest foundation for any future. Your job will be to consistently remind them to maintain a balance in their priorities.

While in the throes of homeschooling our young Motivators, it is vital we have them pause and purposefully invest in others, spend time cultivating their faith, and to remember there is more to life than the goals they are so driven to accomplish. If there was one area of weakness the Motivators might have it would be balance. The great news is, you are their teacher, and you have every day with them to help them turn their weakness into a strength. A passionate, faith-filled Motivator can change the world.

Here are a few ways to help your Motivator to learn a balance in their daily lives.

- Make time in God's Word a priority in their schedule.
- Remind them their faith and knowledge of God's character, promises, and truths will stand when all else fails. Therefore, teach them to bind it about their necks and to carry it with them everywhere.
- Teach them to match their goals to what God wants for their life.

- Teach them that a slower pace or rest doesn't mean apathy or laziness. This is an area in which the Motivator may feel unproductive and undisciplined. Help them build a practice of rest into their day and emphasize the benefits God has in this.

Here are some biblical truths to share with the Motivator:

- "So, whether you eat or drink, or whatever you do, do all to the glory of God." (1 Cor. 10:31)
- "Whatever you do, work heartily, as for the Lord and not for men." (Col. 3:23)
- "Do not be slothful in zeal, be fervent in spirit, serve the Lord." (Rom. 12:11)
- "The beginning of wisdom is this: Get wisdom, and whatever you get, get insight." (Prov. 4:7)

## THE DAWDLERS

If you have a child who dawdles, there is no elaborate description needed. Homeschooling a Dawdler requires patience and understanding. From a complete unawareness of time to a purposeful avoidance of what is in front of them, the Dawdler will need a lot of motivating. The pressure to succeed means nothing to them. The stress of the assignment, the goal, or the work required often precedes and predicts if this child will find something "better" to do with their time. Time is irrelevant and goals are not the force to push them to the end.

Dawdlers are smart and can finish strong. They are motivated by time-sensitive deadlines and the knowledge and power the ownership their decisions have for their life. They thrive when they realize they are on their own and not accountable to another person's timeline or expectations. The pressure of credits and classes and the expectations to get it all done to graduate in a certain period will only suffocate their effectiveness. They are called the Dawdlers because time is irrelevant to them. Sometimes, the responsibility needs to be put into their own hands. When the Dawdler is forced to be accountable to their own attention span and pace, they are more aware of how they work and operate toward a set goal. This may look like failure or repeated efforts, but the Dawdler does well with understanding the consequences of their lack of focus and often just needs a few tools to help them manage their distractions.

The Dawdler thrives with options and alternate schedules or approaches. Confinement and a highly structured environment will stifle their creativity and motivation. Learning to work for and with your child in this capacity is key to them making the grade. It will look different and may even be slower, but it is possible, and it is our job to never give up on finding solutions.

Here are a few ways to empower Dawdlers to make the grade:

- Give them options for classes and a timeline.
- Eliminate distractions but give them the tools for better time management.
- Lists, lists, lists. Dawdlers function best on small, incremental steps and detailed lists.
- Set the goal with them and work backward. Dawdlers work best knowing the end goal, and they usually surprise us by setting a pace to get there.

- Identify areas of distraction or time wasters where they get stuck.

Dawdlers are often simultaneously overwhelmed and under-whelmed. As their homeschool mama, we have a hard job of mo-tivating them with goals and yet also teaching them to be good stewards of all that God has given them. A firm grasp on steward-ship and responsibility to own our strengths, weaknesses, time, and accountability will be their best tools taught in the years you have with them. Integrating time management, scheduled devo-tional times, and accountability into your homeschool will equip your children for the long haul. We often shy away or forget the importance of character and faith development when home-schooling because we are hyper-focused on fitting in all the aca-demics, and quite honestly, sometimes the areas we avoid are the most work for us as well.

A child's faith-filled understanding of ownership and steward-ship is fundamentally life-changing. When they realize and are reminded of God's care and kindness toward us, how He has equipped us all uniquely for His purpose and using our time to steward those gifts well, the pressure of guilt or tasks for motiva-tion falls off your shoulders and into their faith and walk with the Lord. Homeschooling a Dawdler can double our work if we allow it to. We tend to take on the load of work and worry for them, and we get in the way of the words of Jesus, in truth and the power of the Spirit to convict, and move them to own their lives. The Daw-dler's journey in homeschooling may appear to be laziness in their academics, but beneath the surface it is a heart and faith journey.

Here are some biblical truths to share with the Dawdler:

- "Do not be slothful in zeal, be fervent in spirit, serve the Lord." (Rom. 12:11)
- "Whatever your hand finds to do, do it with your might, for there is no work or thought or knowledge or wisdom in Sheol, to which you are going." (Eccl. 9:10)

## THE DOUBTERS

The hesitation to try anything new or to see value in their individuality are the top two markers for the Doubter. As opportunities arise and you expose your child to new and inspiring homeschool, academic, and enrichment activities, they shy away from the first step of trying. Shyness or an introverted nature doesn't always define these students. Instead, they possess a strong hesitation to try because they doubt the potential of their own success. Often, we diagnose this as a lack of courage or fear when really it is an identity issue within themselves and your homeschool.

The Doubters could easily be at the top of their class or be the strong leaders you see they are capable of being, but the hesitation and insecurities keep them from stepping into something they are very capable of doing. When left unchecked at an early age, the Doubter will grow to learn this habit of questioning every little thing, and when it is time to make the grade, the mountain of uncertainty you both will face will feel insurmountable. Doubt leads to indecision, and this is the opposite of our ultimate goal in homeschooling our children.

Raising a Doubter will be a work of the heart and mind and calling out the gifts and identity of strengths in your child without creating a false sense of humility. Once these children trade a habit of insecurity and recognize their voice of confidence, they grow to be more comfortable and secure in their future. Otherwise, they will question every decision and the ability to make the decisions.

The strength of the Doubter is their ability to define what they enjoy, like, or would be interested in pursuing. Their strengths are generally obvious and sometimes hidden, hence the need to try new things. The Doubter will predictably shine when they try something and they succeed, which in turn is enough confidence for them to do it again. They generally thrive once they move past their doubts and believe, but they need the proof from their effort.

Here are a few ways to empower Doubters to make the grade:

- Encourage them to try new things even when it is hard. The saying "confidence is won" has never been truer.
- Learn to identify where the doubts are coming from and to use truth to dispel those thoughts.
- Give them a concrete plan chosen with explanation and reasoning.
- Give them the tools to make bold, confident decisions.
- Allow them to work through planning and owning their choices.

Doubters want to be confident in their work and decisions. Somewhere along the way, Doubters have developed a belief system that mistakes are not allowed and that perfection is supreme. This is a practical and spiritual journey for our children in our homeschool. As they show up for assignments, sports, clubs, co-ops, and friend groups, their ideology should be cemented in the truth of what God says about them and their circumstances. As a homeschooling mom to a Doubter, it will be helpful for you to look for patterns for frustration, internalizations, reactions, or defeat when our children make mistakes in their work, cannot figure something out immediately, or won't try something new for a fear of failure.

Remind your child that the Lord, your home, and you do not require or expect perfection. Listen to your words as you teach or correct. Point them to the words of Scripture that tell us all how we are to try and work and how it is not in vain. Doubters may even doubt their identity in Christ, which in turn affects their thinking. Homeschooling confident kids seems to be one of the fruits of homeschooling. This isn't by accident. By spending time focusing on their identity in Christ and not finding accolades, applause, or gratification solely in accomplishments, but remembering who helps us make good, better, or best. The Doubter gets stuck in their own works and value outside of God's creation and provision of who they were made to be and how God has equipped them.

While homeschooling the Doubter, remind them daily of how to lean into listening to God and what He has for them. Give them the tools to study and understand how God not only instructs us to trust Him but encourages us to lean wholly into Him with our insecurities and doubts. Remind them through their work that perfection can be a conflict of excellence and pride and the Lord just asks and requires us to give back what He has enabled and equipped us to do and nothing more.

Here are some biblical truths to share with the Dawdler:

- "Commit to the LORD whatever you do, and he will establish your plans." (Prov. 16:3 NIV)

- "From the end of the earth I call to you when my heart is faint. Lead me to the rock that is higher than I." (Ps. 61:2)
- "For God gave us a spirit not of fear but of power and love and self-control." (2 Tim. 1:7)

## THE ENTREPRENEURS

Lord, bless the homeschooling moms of Entrepreneurs. Raising and teaching creatives earns you a long vacation from the task of keeping your child focused, while allowing their creative and wandering minds and talents to try new things. Homeschooling an Entrepreneur requires a constant reminder that they will be okay, no matter what. Whether it takes the form of a lemonade stand, a jewelry-making enterprise, or a lawn-care business, the Entrepreneur will use their noticeable gifts and talents and will research, study, learn, and try new things to turn a profit.

The Entrepreneur will struggle to focus on core academics. This isn't a lack of intelligence or capability, but the distraction caused by a flow of ideas and their need for multiple creative outlets. You will notice that when they show up to do their work each day, they see it as "putting in their time." Homeschooling an Entrepreneur requires an understanding of how many other options exist in the learning world outside of the boxed curriculum that arrives at your doorstep and remembering the bookwork can be stifling to an Entrepreneur. We are aware of their need to learn formative core subjects each year, and it is our job to make sure they fit that in. In the long run, however, we'll also need to train them in time and money management, social communication, business plans and excellence, people skills, strong work, moral ethics, and staying committed to what they begin.

Entrepreneurs are idea generators, researchers, eager to execute a plan and to work outside the box or building of this modern-day world. They are visionaries or creatives that absolutely need to use this energy daily or their schoolwork suffers. Their daily home-school schedule should include time for this outlet, and your long-haul journey should give them goals and something exciting to work toward. The Entrepreneur will need a willing ear to listen and sometimes a firm voice to rein in their ideas to a slow and steady path, versus the desire to feel the instant fulfillment of their idea. Don't worry about your Entrepreneur unless you are struggling with their focus and attention where it is needed. This will be your biggest daily struggle. But long-term? No worries for the Entrepreneur. They are going to be just fine, or even better. Their ideas will turn into something great. Just you watch!

Here are a few ways to empower Entrepreneurs to make the grade:

- Learn to match their strongest skill sets with their ideas.
- Be prepared to train and learn areas of weaknesses to support their strengths.
- Try many things and work hard to execute a slow plan.
- Don't rush ideas to feel success; train and work out the bugs.
- Keep them busy and focused.

Homeschooling an Entrepreneur has its highs and lows. Their academics may go through seasons of suffering and peaks of success. Their unpredictability becomes almost predictable. Your job to keep them always centered on their faith, regardless of the highs and lows will be worth investing into your one-on-one time with them, mixed with their academics and their creative outlets. Creatives are passionate people and wherever their focus lands for a time is where their affections, time, attention, and devotion also land. This is wonderful for any required homeschooling assignments, but their gaze and pursuit of a new purpose or passion will always be around the corner. I've raised a houseful of Entrepreneurs, and the best advice and encouragement I can give you is to teach them to know and lean into Christ as their center because their world is full of dreams and options, and God will honor those who use their lives for Him.

Here are some biblical truths for the Entrepreneur:

- "Therefore, my beloved brothers, be steadfast, immovable, always abounding in the work of the Lord, knowing that in the Lord your labor is not in vain." (1 Cor. 15:58)
- "Each of you should use whatever gift you have received to serve others, as faithful stewards of God's grace in its various forms." (1 Peter 4:10 NIV)

### THE LATE BLOOMERS

Better late than never has never been more accurate. The Late Bloomers get a bad rap, especially in the homeschooling world. Not every child knows what they want to do "when they grow up" or has the interest in discovering all their options right out the gate. Homeschooling Late Bloomers takes a mix of gentle and firm resolution to keep their learning on pace and recognizing not everyone is going to have a fast race to the finish line. The Late Bloomers often need a different pace than their peers, less pressure, but encouragement to try new experiences out of their comfort zone. This helps narrow down the passage they need to travel through, so when they are ready to launch, the choices are right before them, and they take right off.

The Late Bloomers are usually not in a hurry but have a firm and almost stubborn resolve to choose a path when they are ready. Take caution to not allow this resolve to halt progress, growth, or finishing strong. Every year of homeschooling a Late Bloomer will require a foreknowledge and awareness that they may seem "behind," but they will catch up. Their lack of hurriedness can be a gift of calm and peace in your own homeschooling journey, often giving us one less thing to think about, but in all honesty, we should be careful to not let their slower pace keep us from equipping them to finish strong.

The Late Bloomers have depth and a perception of the future hidden in the recesses of their thoughts toward school and growth. Whether this manifests itself as disinterest, learning challenges, or perhaps fear of the unknown when their school at home journey comes to an end, we can help alleviate their fears with a plan to help them finish strong.

Here are a few traits of the Late Bloomers:

Consistency—their biggest strength
Awareness of what is required but need a plan and a pace set
    for them and with them
Unaware of their definitive strengths and need more time to
    explore, navigate, and choose

Show up when needed

Take assignments and goals seriously and are independent
workers

I encourage you to let the Late Bloomer set their pace and fill
in the spaces they have with moments of discovery of their interests and solidify those with incremental plans. Idle time is an
enemy to progress and growth. The Late Bloomer may often get
discouraged with their indecision to their interests, goals, or progress. Perseverance will be the key character quality you will bring
before them in reminding them of the Lord's plan and purpose
for their life. If the Late Bloomer is not taught to remember there
is always a plan for their life, they will become discouraged in the
comparison trap. We all know that comparison is the thief of joy.

Homeschooling the Late Bloomer will give you a window into
their heart and an opportunity to infuse truth into the cracks that
will fold together in time. Reminding them they are God's child,
and they are not forgotten even when they are not doing or growing where and when everyone else is.

Here are some biblical truths for the Late Bloomer:

- "But one thing I do: forgetting what lies behind and straining forward to what lies ahead, I press on toward the goal
  for the prize of the upward call of God in Christ Jesus."
  (Phil. 3:13–14)
- "I am sure of this, that he who began a good work in you
  will bring it to completion at the day of Jesus Christ."
  (Phil. 1:6)

*personal reflection*

It takes time and deep heart and character work to homeschool different children in the way they should go.

*personal challenge*

I will take the time to know what motivates my child for their future. I will put off guilt as a motivator and lean into the uniqueness in my own child and stop comparing them to the expectations of the world or those around me.

*drawing from the well*

God knows the plans He has for my children. His Word planted in their lives will reap fruit. I can trust His unfailing love and promises even when I may get it wrong.

*"Blessed is the one who trusts in the LORD, whose confidence is in him. They will be like a tree planted by the water that sends out its roots by the stream. It does not fear when heat comes; its leaves are always green. It has no worries in a year of drought and never fails to bear fruit."*
Jeremiah 17:7–8 NIV

*a prayer for my homeschool*

Father God, I come to You today in confidence, knowing You created my child with an amazing and unique learning style, gifts, and personality. Give me eyes to see, wisdom to teach, and a heart to love the parts of our journey where I feel frustrated, don't understand, or feel like we are hitting roadblocks. I am trusting in Your plan. In Jesus' name, Amen.

*chapter 17*

- - · · · - - · · - - - · - - · · · -

# The Long Haul

*E*ach season of homeschooling will feel and look different. We will face new temptations and new encouragements. Preparing ourselves for the long haul is paramount. We usually focus on classes, requirements, schedules, and all the external pieces, but a successful homeschool is not a hurried homeschool. You've seen the hurried homeschooler before. Maybe you even identify with this and think there is no way to successfully finish well. The distance from point A to point B can be long, and so it is vital we are prepared for the pace. There is no such thing as instant homeschool success. Don't rush your child's pace to the finish line. They will feel pressed in from all sides, struggling to keep up, and will learn a habit of hurry is normal, forgetting the most valuable life lessons along the way.

Our children are not supposed to be products of a system. We chose homeschooling so we could set their pace and not track with a group of learners on different levels and schedules. We chose homeschooling to teach them life lessons and give them a grasp on fundamental character and to grow face-to-face relationships with them and to build on how God created them. When we hurry ahead of God's plan, we can forget what He has given us and how far He has brought us. We keep our eyes so set on the end that we pick up our pace to finish faster. We all need a remedy to the hurried pace to the finish line.

*An unhurried homeschool gives us time*
*to pace our learning and finish well.*

I am often reminded of the Israelites in the book of Exodus. God rescued them in their time of need. They spent forty years wandering in the desert, and God met them in their times of greatest fear and uncertainty. Right from the start, they weren't taking the easy and fastest route. They were led through hot, dry, and barren wasteland. Their grumblings began almost immediately. But God promised them it would be worth fighting for; going the distance would be full of blessing. Their faith would be stretched, and they would have to depend on God like never before.

As the Israelites approached the Red Sea, it must have looked bigger and deeper the closer they got. Their eyes became focused on the magnitude of the challenge in front of them, and they forgot His faithfulness. But God didn't forget about them. He split the seas in two, and He made a way. He always makes a way. Even if the way He is leading us through is the last thing we ever thought we would do, we can always trust Him. When we take our eyes off God, we become fixated on the end of the journey, and the path leading us there becomes excruciatingly long and sometimes, unbearable.

*Our homeschool journey is also a faith journey.*

Scripture tells us in Exodus 13:17–18 that, "When Pharaoh let the people go, God did not lead them by way of the land of the Philistines, although that was near. For God said, 'Lest the people change their minds when they see war and return to Egypt.' But God led the people around by the way of the wilderness toward the Red Sea."

God knows we will face struggles, want to change course, hide on the difficult days, and even give up. He wants us to keep moving forward, remembering He is with us and guiding us along the way. Forty years is a long time to trust, follow, wait, and to show up when you're in the desert. God continued to be with His people, just as He is with you and me daily. There are no hidden places from Him in our hearts and minds where He cannot work and make a way. The years we homeschool may prove to be the most faith-building times for us and our families, but we may not see His faithfulness until we have reached the finish line.

You may feel as if you have sacrificed a lot and will never see the end of this journey. Your homeschooling may have dry, boring seasons or struggles you never anticipated. You have been stretched and your faith has been tested, but I want to give you this hopeful reminder that the way to our promised land is not always easy—it rarely is. But it's worth it. God is faithful and will bring goodness to your efforts as you surrender the journey as you go.

Consider the ways in which the long homeschooling journey will be worth the effort and time.

## THE LONG HAUL PRECIPITATES SUCCESS

I look back and consider the three decades I have been homeschooling and can say without a doubt, if the journey had been short, sweet, and easy, my reliance on God would have been minimized to the bumps in the road and my efforts would have never changed. The difficult days and the winding learning curves are where I learned to put my trust in a God who faithfully led me out of the desert to rivers of water. Had I given up or become apathetic, this next generation would not have seen and experienced for themselves the fruit of pressing on.

When I consider the route the Israelites took to get to the promised land, I think of the words "the long way around." It was not a direct route, but the Lord had purpose in this. He knew if they faced battle after battle in the beginning of their journey, they would give up before they even started. God brings clarity and defined purpose in long journeys. He has solidified my determination, my fortitude, my perseverance, and most of all, my faith.

The success of my homeschool is not all wrapped up in the best grades or scholarships. I count it a win when I can say thank you for the hard times and watch my older children thrive in the areas that seemed to be the longest and hardest parts of our journeys. The years have borne fruit that could not have been grown without pruning and praying in the longest stretches of our homeschooling years. There is fruit from perseverance. You will see it in your children's decisions. The daily investments of time you spent teaching them math or spelling, while juggling your home and relationships and work, they saw your investment as commitment, and this is success.

Children who learn fortitude and perseverance at home carry this into their adult lives successfully. There is fruit in diligence. It will show up in the hard work and school they continue when they leave home for college, their careers, or their families. A home-schooled child sees the sweat and tears and the showing up all day, every day for the long haul. It wasn't always easy, but the success of showing up day after day bears fruit when they leave our homes, and we know they will be okay because they were taught diligence for a long time. There is fruit in excellence. You not only decided to take the long road of homeschooling with your children, but your work in calling your children up to their fullest potential is a pursuit of excellence.

The world defines success at different levels, from money, professional résumé, property, awards—the list is endless. It really is all about perspective. None of those successful goals are wrong in themselves. Perhaps in the pursuit of external success in our homeschooling or raising our children, we may have forgotten the true purpose of the long journey.

*Homeschooling teaches us more about ourselves*
*and a faithful God and less about the destination.*

I've created a short list for you to refer to when you are creating goals for your child for this long haul. Not only are these goals, but they are also encouraging benchmarks for you to refer to and remember as you reach the finish line. After all of the bookwork and future plans are discussed and accomplished, this list will give you the long-range perspective that you have indeed succeeded.

Write this list in your personal journal for your homeschooling child to help you remain assured in the future.

- Responsible, hard-working, well-balanced adults who love Jesus
- Children (young or old) who understand stewardship and honor
- Living a life defined by perseverance and steadfastness
- Understanding perfection and worldly accolades will not fulfill
- Adjustment and adaptation to an educational or vocational world
- Understanding job, ministry, service, and their calling all as life work

Let's be careful not to relegate success to our measure of growth and achievement. We are wise to remember the growth, sanctification, and redemption we cannot see or measure. We do not know the work God is doing beneath the surface of outward goals and achievements. As parents, it is good to remember God allows us to be instruments and stewards of our children's lives, but really, He is filling in the gaps and has a plan we cannot see or comprehend as the finished work of Christ in our children's lives. It takes time, and sometimes this means waiting and casting off fear of failure. And when you find yourself worrying if they will ever "succeed," or wonder if you have failed them, remember the measure of success is not ours to see or give.

## THE LONG HAUL PRODUCES HUMILITY

Just when the Israelites were "rescued" from their plight, they reached a new and yet more arduous part of their journey, quickly forgetting the goodness of the Lord. We read about their complaining and grumbling as they were met with hardship and realized the length of their journey. They became loud and ungrateful. To us reading today, it is obvious and despairing that they couldn't be thankful or humble to receive the blessings God promised them. We acknowledge how quickly they seemed to forget. It didn't take them long to begin making their own plans, in their own strength and might. As the reader of this biblical account, we are shocked and can see what was to come. We want to speak back in time or through the pages and tell them to wait, listen, and learn. To not lean on their own understanding. To trust in the Lord. To be slow to speak and quick to listen. To let the Lord their God be their guide and their provider.

Our homeschooling journey can and will produce humility. Humble surrender of our perfected plans and micromanagement of what our children will do or become begins at the dawn of every morning, in the middle of a frustrating or difficult math lesson (can you tell this was a source of continual surrender in my home?). There may be moments your child will do or say something that blaringly shines a spotlight on your homeschooling weaknesses. I encourage all homeschooling moms to find the balance between "not knowing anything and walking slowly in confidence" as they homeschool. Homeschooling without humility will only leave room for anger and gaps in our teaching and homes that reap frustration and regret. Humility isn't something we can "put on" with a quiet voice or a discouraged spirit. Humility isn't a bad thing or something to fear that will leave you depressed or low. Humility is a virtue we grow in daily and it grows room in our lives for the Holy Spirit to use our lives to show God's glory.

Below are some ways to homeschool with humility:

- Put off feelings of offense when you feel the sting of awareness or conviction.
- Recognize your personal areas of weakness and show up to make the changes necessary.
- Realize you will not be able to control the outcome.
- Learn not to micromanage every part of your child's life.
- Allow others to speak wisdom into your life.
- Ask questions.

## THE LONG HAUL REVEALS OUR HEARTS

Oh, how our hearts are exposed in the middle of a long, challenging journey. Homeschooling is certainly not a "woe is me" commitment but will have its trying seasons. The testing of my faith has revealed pieces of my heart that I'd never seen before and the hearts and lives of my family as well. You never really know your family until you spend 24/7 with them, until they leave home. All day, every day may be an exaggeration, but the hours reveal so many layers to who we are. Even with the best intentions, the worst in us can be exposed.

I would love to say my homeschooling journey was adorned with sweet, magical moments and laced with quiet music, learning, and time in the Word every day. Those are parts of homeschooling I was purposeful in and made some of the most beautiful memories. Homeschooling revealed more of me than I ever knew it could. It felt ugly to be face to face with my reaction to a lack of control, fear, or even the impatience that would come with teaching multiple children for many years. "I don't blame you," some would say. If I were to go back and share heart checks with myself, I would have been more aware at how desperate I was for a healthy heart attitude in my homeschooling.

*Healthy Homeschool Heart Checks*

- Do I react quickly to inconvenience?

- Do I have an attitude of resentment or envy for those not homeschooling?

- Do I feel my struggle is so great, I have no hope?

- Do I give up when the going gets tough?

- Where do my affections or comforts lie when I feel discouraged?

- Do my reactions or decisions reflect everyone's interests or just mine?

## THE LONG HAUL FORTIFIES OUR HOMES

If there was ever a topic of transformation and testimony on how homeschooling truly changes you and your home from the inside out, it would be the long haul! Our home would absolutely not be the way it is today if we had not homeschooled. I have witnessed an incredible generational shift in family dynamics and the transformation of our home and life because we had the time. Because we had so much intentional time and teaching in our home—communication, virtues, personal identity, work ethic— the ceiling my husband and I had in our earlier years has become our children's floor. They have been given so much more training and time than we ever had. They can build upon the foundation we have established.

Time and intentionality will reap a harvest of blessing if you use your homeschooling for daily investments. Homeschooling fortified our home in the way we communicate with one another. Our children not only received an education but also learned one another's learning and communication styles. They learned to be patient in the process of one another's growth and approach to problems, giving space and growing in grace where someone else didn't have the same strengths. Our home functioned as "one body," utilizing the different parts in giftings and strengths. We were fortified in prayer as we shared trials and struggles together. We learned compassion for those hurting or needing help. Our home was fortified because we learned how to love one another well.

*Fortifying Your Homeschooling Home*

- Put Jesus at the center of all you do.
- Remember that everything you teach and do together now will be the cornerstone that supports our family in the future.
- Pressing into hard moments together as a family will not feel or look normal but will create a bond of trust for the future.
- When one struggles, everyone supports.

###### ······· *personal reflection* ·······

In what way has the end goal distracted you from seeing and knowing God is right by your side? In what ways can you enjoy your home-school journey today and to the finish line?

###### ······· *personal challenge* ·······

I will keep the long-term goal in mind and enjoy the moments we have on this journey. I will set up goal posts or truth in each season reminding me of the very good work and worth we are investing. I will teach my children the Word daily.

###### ······· *drawing from the well* ·······

Like medicine to a sick body, the Word and the conviction of the Holy Spirit can make us whole and healthy. Without Jesus at the center of our homeschooling, we will continue for the long haul, but trying to do it in our own strength.

> *"For no one can lay a foundation other than that which is laid, which is Jesus Christ."* 1 Corinthians 3:11

> *"Everyone then who hears these words of mine and does them will be like a wise man who built his house on the rock. And the rain fell, and the floods came, and the winds blew and beat on that house, but it did not fall, because it had been founded on the rock. And everyone who hears these words of mine and does not do them will be like a foolish man who built his house on the sand. And the rain fell, and the floods came, and the winds blew and beat against that house, and it fell, and great was the fall of it."* Matthew 7:24–27

*a prayer for my homeschool*

Lord, I want to live my life for You. Help me stay committed to this calling with hope and perseverance, teaching my children of Your Word and truth, that all our days will give You the glory, even in my weakness. In Jesus' name, Amen.

*chapter 18*

## - - · · -•-•-•- - ·•· - -

# Teamwork Makes
# the Dream Work

*I*t has been three decades since my two oldest school-aged
children, two babies, and I sat at our small kitchen table, with
our dream to homeschool. My husband and I and our four kids
were "the team." Dan and I raised our children, taught them what
we knew and what we didn't know, worked in sync in the evenings, and tag-teamed during the day. We homeschooled in many
small and inconvenient spaces, living in different places. Everywhere we planted our family, we grew in wisdom and solidarity.
Our family grew and this meant more work and learning more
about homeschooling multiple children and raising them in balance with a healthy, joy-filled home.

It was vital for us to not let homeschooling become our whole
life or "who we were"; instead, we wanted it to be an extension of
learning in our home. The joy of watching my children learn has
brought me the greatest blessings . . . and continues to. We grew up
together, and although I was the homeschooling mom, we were all

one team, rooting for one another, helping one another, and troubleshooting how to make things better, easier, or best for one another. As I reflect on this, I see we still function like this today. We are still "team strong." I couldn't have dreamed it could work out this way. Finding your people is necessary. Growing a team is vital.

I did not do this alone. Absolutely no way, no how. No one can or should homeschool alone. When I think of the community, the people, those we fostered relationships with over the years, I think back to the place and purpose each one has had a part in our homeschooling career. When my children graduate, I reach out to those formative people, motivators, encouragers, mentors, and influencers and ask them to write a letter to the graduate. Each note is written as a personal challenge, with words of encouragement to continue pressing on, while also calling up their abilities and gifts and acknowledging their work and worth in God. The letters and notes are a surprise for the graduate. I collect them, tuck them in their scrapbook or box of cherished memories, along with their awards and papers with smiley face or star stickers I selectively saved from the endless worksheets we did together. Then I present them at their graduation party.

The long journey also brings life full circle. Remember those naysayers at the beginning of your homeschooling journey? They either grew weary of their efforts or have become your biggest encouragers.

As first-generation homeschoolers, we had to define what teamwork would look like for our family. We grew a family, saved, and purchased and cleared land, built our home from the ground up, board by board, wall by wall. We worked to build a home and give them an education which far surpassed all our time around books and studies. As they build their lives and homeschool their own children, I watch the same principles we instilled and lived out continue in this next generation. Teamwork does make the dream work.

## FAMILY MATTERS

You may not have extended family or friends who understand why you are homeschooling, and therefore, you may not have the support system you need. Remember that you have one another. You have the gift to create a team within your home that will stand the test of time, but this is going to take work. Families are conditioned to function *in* the same home, but not *for* one another. The fast-paced lives of families in today's culture can be overwhelming, and it may seem impossible to create a rhythm that sanctions togetherness, helpfulness, and teamwork.

Just as any community, workplace, or ministry needs some structure to thrive and grow, a family will need some of this framework to achieve a level of excellence and value. We've always told our children that anything of worth is worth working for. The key to a homeschooling team framework is respect and honor. Everyone in your family will have a different ideal studying or learning environment. Respecting others' time for studying can be challenging in a home with many people.

Work schedules will require flexibility and will give us opportunities to put others before ourselves. Knowing and remembering how God created us all uniquely and with gifts is a necessary part of raising children who think, not of their own needs only, but of the needs of others. We don't want to raise consumers.

*Let's raise kids who see others for who God made them*
*to be rather than what they can do for them.*

A homeschooling mom can end up in burnout if she tries to manage and do it all. A family dynamic of consideration, helpfulness, bearing one another's burdens, deference, and respect will not only disperse the load of responsibility, but nurture honor, respect, time management, and responsibility. This transition can often be a more difficult transition than the homeschooling of our children. We ease into teaching because we are the teacher, and the kids show up to do the "expected schoolwork" each day. But when we try and disperse household responsibilities to everyone to share the burden, we often hold tight to the roles because the temptation to micromanage or oversee every task is more work than just doing it ourselves.

*Being a team leader is yet another hat homeschooling moms*
*need to wear to make the dream work.*

Evaluation and delegation will be your best tools for successful family teamwork. Consider the areas in your homeschooling where you are "expendable." As mentioned previously, delegate those areas to independent work, outsourced tutoring, or community co-op classes. Evaluate the areas of your home undone at the end of the day or specific jobs you can share or delegate to your family, which will equip them for when they leave home. Create a buddy system for your school schedule. Pair an older child with another to practice spelling words, rotate lunch duty, someone to clean up the breakfast kitchen or to do dictation lessons with a sibling. As moms, we often have a hard time with delegation because we may feel as if we aren't giving our children "our all," or that homeschooling is all about us doing all the things.

Loosen your grip on perfection or control and allow your family to help you. Teaching your children how to do their new jobs well is going to take time and effort. The follow-up may seem like more work than doing it yourself. Don't lose heart, for the best is yet to come. These are those moments everyone talks about when we say homeschooling is more than just bookwork.

*Homeschooling is character work, heart work, and housework.*

## HOMESCHOOL COMMUNITY

If there is any reason to join a homeschool community, co-op, or support group, consider the future and not your present circumstances. There will be a day you will say or think, "I wish we had more support." Your children will either grow to resent the isolation, or in hindsight tell you they wish they had more friends or socialization. Most of us have found those sweet spaces and discovered the hidden treasures of a community. It takes time to discover the right homeschool community. A common misconception I have observed in the homeschool world is that everyone within a homeschool community is going to be in 100 percent alignment with your homeschooling approach, belief systems, and family styles. If we wait around for the perfect match, we may never enjoy and reap the fruit and benefits of being part of a people group with the same end goal, but different approaches.

Unrealistic expectations and standards will affect our children in ways you cannot see right now. They'll see a critical spirit, pride, isolation, and preference over the greater need of community, help, support, friendships, and encouragement. Surely, we don't want to yoke ourselves with a belief system in the homeschool world that would affect our children in their foundations of faith, but there is a big difference between a different faith and different homeschool approaches. When we find ourselves niching ourselves and our family into the "one way" of homeschooling and have trouble fellowshipping with others, we should watch over our hearts.

The gift of fellowshipping with other homeschooling families is more far-reaching than the occasional co-op or enrichment get-togethers. Finding a community will give you a fresh perspective, new ideas, friendships, support for the hard days, new sources for materials and tutors, class suggestions, or teaching approaches. Let's be honest, we search out communities for our children, but in the end, *we* also win. As much as we find it difficult to break away from our scheduled homeschool plan or lists of undone housework or errands (which always come last), once we engage in our communities, we are so thankful for the respite and gift of like-minded gatherings. If this sounds too good to be true, I'd encourage you to either find your people or start a group today.

*Every successful idea is born from a need,*
*and we all need community!*

## HIDDEN STRENGTHS AND GIFTS

Homeschool mama, I want to ask you to pause here. Read the next words, and silently sit with them for a time. These words are for you and you only. Ask yourself this question: "What gifts or strengths do I possess, have stopped using, or have never used with or in front of my family?" Ponder and write out your list before moving on. I know you have more than one thing that came to your mind and if not, maybe this will help.

I found this time of introspection to be a helpful shift in my perspective. I found great delight in teaching science to my children because I have always enjoyed studying how God created the world so intricately. My passion to see His intelligent design in the hidden things of this world drove me to learn more and teach my children this subject with more passion. I discovered the hidden strength of leadership in ministry circles because the Lord gifted me with ten children to teach, lead, and love.

Oh, how this prepared me for so many future opportunities. Not until I took the time to identify the gifts and strengths I have did I truly embrace and apply those to our homeschooling. I began to find other outlets of enjoyable pursuit that paired with my interests. Often, we have obvious jobs we do every day, but there is always something else about us that is hidden from the world and possibly even ourselves that we haven't shared or put to use. When you find those secret places, write out what you would like to learn, study, and have always dreamed or wanted to know more about, experience, or try.

Making a list of your passions on paper will help your family begin to see you bloom and grow in areas that bring you joy; it will teach them we are to be lifelong learners. Not only will this give you an outlet of discovery and learning, but you will begin to share this with others, the first of which is your family. This is another valuable life lesson for our children to know we have something more to offer than "just being their mom and teacher." They are inspired by determination, learning new things, and in turn showing them how to foster skills, growth and sharing those with the world. Isn't that what homeschooling is about? If you cannot find the time to do this, then re-create the wheel and framework of schedules in your home to make this a priority. Your new skills and gifts will greatly bless your family and the homeschool community. Never stop growing, learning, and sharing.

*You are the most important person in your homeschool.*
*It is vital you grow and learn as well.*

## MINISTRY AS PART OF HOMESCHOOLING

Homeschooling can have far-reaching effects beyond the walls of your home. The lessons in selflessness and how to loosen up your rigid schedules will allow your family to use their lives for others. We reframe our minds and hearts to remembering our purpose is to glorify God in all we say and do and to love others well. We learn to reprioritize and schedule our homeschooling days with eternity in mind. Once your family has established the framework of teamwork, your schedules will now allow for more time for ministry and areas of service.

Serving and ministry are an extension of your homeschool, a representation of your family, and a testimony of your faith and the gospel. All three of those things are names you and your family carry when you step outside of your homeschool room, and it is notable to carry those names and titles well. The teamwork and character learned in your home will help your family minister to others. There are so many areas of service or ministry we have equipped our children for while homeschooling but using them outside of the home will be new and, perhaps, out of their comfort zone.

*Teaching your children to love one another well in your homeschool will be an overflow to the world and others.*

Every week, from the time our children were little until they graduated, we took weekly visits to the local nursing home. We didn't have a specific loved one we were visiting, but I chose this space to be the place for my children to learn to see others uniquely. It took a great amount of teamwork to get us all out the door and to the nursing home every week. I preempted these visits with daily conversations and activities. For handwriting on a Monday, they would all write a neatly penned letter to a resident. Their artwork was often wrapped in a plastic grocery bag and tied with ribbon for a bed-bound individual.

I taught them chess and checkers and they packed their game boards each week to play with their person of choice. Every time they practiced their piano lesson pages, we pretended we were their future nursing home audience to prepare them for playing for others. Once a week, we would pack homemade baked goods, music books, artwork and letters, games, and some creative brainstorming ideas they eventually came up with on their own, and we would enter a whole new world of loving others well.

My children were afraid of the many different faces, health obstacles, and a new environment when we first began visiting nursing homes. After many weeks of kind encouragement and discussions on our drive home, what had first felt different became normal and our children learned how to serve others. Each of our children "adopted" their own resident, listening to the life stories, writing them down, taking pictures with them, and then creating a special life journal for their new friends.

The differrences, sights, smells, and worry faded away as they poured their time and thoughts into others. Conflicts at home waned as the focus off what they wanted or felt they deserved shifted into time, consideration, and preparation for serving others. Every ounce of teaching in our home was always for more than what it seemed. Every lesson, conversation, and skill was preparing our children to live an abundant life, for themselves and for others.

*Every skill, character lesson, and intentional selfless moment you teach in your homeschool is preparing your children to live in the world with adaptivity and ministry to others and those around them.*

## OUR CLOSEST FRIEND

Even with all the support systems, we will always have a friend who is like no other right by our side—Jesus, our friend who never leaves us and has promised to always be by our side. There will be homeschooling days when the teamwork doesn't work, the community is too much work, and the ministry isn't going to work. Those days and every day, you can step away or sit in the middle of the pile of books, papers, dishes in the sink, and children waiting on you to show up, and you need more than a system to make it all come together.

Our relationship with God in heaven sustains and carries us every day here on earth. He is our ever-present help in trouble. His name means provider, sustainer, comforter, teacher, and friend. When your homeschooling moments become daunting and your family team is on a different page, His promises are still the same.

*······· personal reflection ·······*

Am I teaching my children to love one another and others well?

*······· personal challenge ·······*

List five people you can count on to "be there" in your homeschool-ing journey. Identify areas of your home and subjects in your home-schooling where you need support and find a team or create a new plan to help make the long-haul work for everyone. How is my family serving one another in our homeschool?

*······· drawing from the well ·······*

As I come to the well today, may I remember His promises never run dry. When the work is hard and I find my spirit growing weary, I want to remember I am never alone.

> *"Commit to the LORD whatever you do,*
> *and he will establish your plans."* Proverbs 16:3 NIV

*···· a prayer for my homeschool ····*

Father, I feel You transforming our home and our schooling in a new direction. Help us to continually point our learning and lives toward You. I need creativity and a renewed spirit to cultivate hearts of love and learning in our home. I need You. In Jesus' name, Amen.

# chapter 19

# Have I Failed My Children?

*M*any nights I would fall asleep asking myself the loaded question, "Am I failing my children?" Rolling this question and more around in my head for many years wasted a lot of energy and revealed a lack of faith, and supremely, my attempt at control. I had a strong check of conviction when the Lord showed me that the patterns I had fallen into were an idol of believing I had the sufficiency to not fail my children. We all will fail at homeschooling at one time or another. I know this isn't what you wanted to hear. There are so many opportunities daily to mess up, disappoint our children, and to fail at even our best efforts. The sufficiency of Christ in my life has never been so tangible and held close to me than raising and homeschooling my children.

*We can easily lose our joy when fear crowds the room.*

Even though I have consistently homeschooled our youngest four after our first six children graduated, I held on to my weakest areas and doubts in my home and school and allowed them to speak louder than our victories. I listened to the world's standards and feedback about homeschooled children, felt the failure of meeting those standards, and applied that to my thought patterns. I looked back on my mistakes, changes I have made since, regret over my inability to give 100 percent all the time, my immaturity, and my overcompensation where I was afraid.

I asked my children how they would have described their experiences as they were growing up and how they'd describe them now through the lens of adulthood. Foresight and hindsight are valuable, and I wish someone had shared this with me earlier in my homeschool journey.

Here are a few snippets of real-life homeschooling moments I have lived on repeat with each of my children and onto the next generation with my grandchildren. I reached out to all my children when I was almost done writing this book. All ten of our children were homeschooled and seven of them have graduated and are living their amazing adult lives. I asked them to consider sharing two perspectives on their homeschooling experience with me. Granted, this was a risky move, because homeschooling ten children means ten different personalities and ten different experiences, in addition to mine. I prayerfully decided this would be the best decision for this book, because I want you to be able to see that it will require humility and insight to ask hard questions and to homeschool each child uniquely and to be okay with knowing the outcomes are not in your control.

I asked my children to answer two questions about their homeschooling experiences:

1. While homeschooling, what were your feelings then and how was your experience at that time?
2. Looking back, now that you are an adult with your own family or career, what are your thoughts on homeschooling and your experience?

Here are a few responses from my children:

"Homeschooling I felt like as a kid and adult was a gift. Although I missed the musical theatre and other small opportunities that public school offered, I feel like the pros of homeschooling outweighed it all. I was able to not only learn basic and higher education, but also how to have and grow healthy family relationships, healthy friendships, maintain a house, get creative with free time, and make life-lasting memories. And the cherry on top . . . we started each morning in the most important way—with family devotions. Something I will always be grateful for. I feel like it is so easy to do homeschooling wrong and have seen it happen in the real world, but the difference between great homeschooling with positive effect and negative homeschooling lies at the heart of the teacher/parent. Thankfully my mom poured her whole heart into what she did. And because of that, I wouldn't trade my homeschooling experience for the world."

＊＊ ＊ ＊＊ ⁃

"When I hear the word homeschooling, many things come to mind, but the top two would have to be my home and my siblings. Being homeschooled has meant different things to me as I grow older and means more to me each year. I loved waking up, getting my things ready for the day, and heading up to the schoolroom with all my siblings. Doing school might mean we'd pause to go on walks outside, go on field trips, have co-op with friends, or play in the snow most of the day. I loved getting to learn beside my siblings and hands-on. I also loved how we did devotions as a family before starting our schoolwork for the day, with learning the names of God, the books of the Bible, reading through the Bible each year, memorizing Scripture, and coming up with our own devotions to lead. That's something I've noticed that I took for granted as I talk with my friends who aren't homeschooled and didn't do family devotions like I had. My mom was my teacher; she sat down with each sibling, helping them learn and grasp what she was teaching. She had us all practice different skills, get exercise, learn music, spend time outside, learn to clean the house and make meals, and so much more besides just school. Homeschoolers are often seen as different; less educated, less social, and faced with a lot of challenges when it comes to education. I love homeschooling because it's personal, it's not sitting in classrooms all day, memorizing facts, and getting good grades. It's creative, personal, patient, and fun."

●● ● ● ● -

"While homeschooling, my feelings about it reflected my experience. My homeschooling was structured with flexibility. That created an environment where I could safely build character qualities of respectfulness, confidence, and flexibility.

Morning routines, test taking, charts, art and music studies, and chores were all a part of the structure. This structure helped give me the tools I needed to extend my schooling beyond the home. Not to mention the invaluable Home Ec 'courses' I learned to master. Playing my music for the elderly at a nursing home (becoming more confident and compassionate), practicing my spelling with my siblings in the car (learning to teach and be taught), attending local co-ops (respecting other teachers and navigating peer pressure), cleaning and cooking for the sick (using my skill and knowledge to bless others). The list goes on. I really enjoyed being homeschooled and remember not having any interest in 'going' to school until my mid-teens. The younger years of homeschooling were a beautiful balance of character training, academics, playfulness, and exploring. Did I mention the hours of creativity I had with my siblings in our great woods?"

■ ■ • ■ ■ • -

"I loved my homeschooling experience. I value the one-on-one help and praise that I received in my work—whether excelling in language arts or needing extra help in mathematics. With my firstborn starting pre-K this year, I realized three things can aid a successful and beautiful homeschooling experience: the teacher, community, and resources. My mother is a natural teacher. Yet, she applied herself to homeschooling probably more than any of my siblings have had to. She researched, studied, and outsourced. She helped give us all the necessary tools we needed. We had the opportunities to apply our studies and talents in the community, attend local co-ops, serve our church, perform in recitals, and attend hybrid classes. While I had a good experience with homeschooling, I admit it can be intimidating, despite having a mother with 20+ years' experience and far more resources available to me than she had. But I recognize that intimidation comes from not being on her side of things and from a need to apply myself to the initial hard part of becoming familiar with what is available, and my own children and their tendencies. I've never grown out of homeschooling. I'm still balancing daily living with learning new skills from home!"

━ ● ● ● ● ━

"I think that the community you surround yourself with can play a HUGE role in the success and enjoyment in homeschooling for the parent, and for the child. There were a few years of being homeschooled that I did not enjoy, and a few years of being homeschooled that I knew were so good. When I look back to try to figure out why the feelings, I would ask myself, Was it my age? Was it how hard school was? Nope, it came back to who I was surrounded by. When I was surrounded by other families who had the same values about education and home learning (life skills), and we did life together, or learned together, or it was 'cool' in that circle, then I loved homeschooling. Homeschooling was 'cool.' When I was surrounded by people who didn't homeschool and lived very different lives, a part of me would become discontented with the reality of changing diapers, cooking meals from home, learning from home. Just being . . . home. I understand that our homeschool journey may have been unconventional in that there were 10 of us and it was just as much 'life school' in every moment of life, as it was homeschooled, and that can become a lot. They say practice makes perfect and homeschool was every bit of practice for real life every bit of the time, and I am so thankful to be on the other end, looking back, and realizing all I learned BECAUSE I was homeschooled."

We waffle in the argument between being humble and aware of areas we need help, improvement, or to change in our homeschooling to walking in confidence in the process and learning together. Surrender and wisdom will be your greatest tools for discernment as you work through the dos and don'ts of homeschooling.

We have set a standard we ourselves feel compelled to live up to. *We must work diligently to remain steadfast in being prepared to homeschool our children in excellence.* There are many biblical truths tied up in this statement. Learning to filter all our fears, worries, expectations—and, yes, even failures—through the lens of Scripture is the only peace-filled way to humbly face our choice to homeschool our children.

*For each doubt you put off, remember to replace with a biblical truth.*

======= *personal reflection* =======

### Four Don'ts

Don't leave Jesus out of your homeschool.
Don't be a hypocrite.
Don't forget to listen to your children.
Don't forget you will make mistakes.

### Four Dos

Point to the gospel in everything you do and teach.
Pray and seek wisdom and counsel.
Stay focused on the goal.
Be accountable.

======= *personal challenge* =======

Where do I struggle with fear and control? I will thank God for the beautiful blessing that is my family. I will pray I can find contentment and peace.

======= *drawing from the well* =======

Fear is the biggest component of failure. When we bring our homeschooling to the Lord in prayer, worship, and humility, the Lord can change us, grow us, and meet our children where they are without us fearing what we may be missing. God loves our children more than even we do. He is capable to helping, guiding, and filling in the gaps we may feel we are lacking in. There is a peace that dispels fear when we remember God's all-encompassing love.

> "For I, the LORD your God, hold your right hand; it is I who say
> to you, 'Fear not, I am the one who helps you.'" Isaiah 41:13

*···· a prayer for my homeschool ····*

Father, I started this journey for my children and here I am before You in need of your grace and wisdom even more than the day we began. Thank You for my children, our homeschooling, and the blessings I often forget to see in a day, because I am blinded by fear. In Jesus' name, Amen.

*chapter 20*

- • • - • • - • - • - • - • • -

# Checking the Boxes

The top two questions we ask ourselves at the end of every year until we finish homeschooling our children are, "Did we give them everything they needed?" and "Did we miss anything?" Don't worry, you are not alone in wondering if you have checked all the boxes. Every homeschool checklist will be different, but as we head into the homestretch, I need to share this with you.

Out of all the classes and top grades your child accomplishes, we should be careful not to forget a few life lessons and foundational areas they need to know each year and beyond. In contrast, this list is universal and is often missed because we are so focused on making the grade. We have more than enough hours in a day to train our children in the way they should go, and this includes guiding them in truth, life skills, and concepts unto the Lord. We have been called to train them as we sit, lie, stand, and walk:

*And these words that I command you today shall be on your heart. You shall teach them diligently to your children, and shall talk of them when you sit in your house, and when you walk by*

*the way, and when you lie down, and when you rise. You shall*
*bind them as a sign on your hand, and they shall be as frontlets*
*between your eyes.* (Deut. 6:6–8)

Whether your children are tykes or teens, it is never too late to begin building their academic portfolios with their future in mind, life skills, relationships, character, and studying God's Word together. Remember, you have been called to this and it may never be convenient, so be sure to make the time.

## ACADEMICS

Every state has different homeschooling requirements, so the accountability for compiling a portfolio will vary. Following standards set for us in the listing of required courses and hours isn't always a bad thing. Many times, we may see this as stifling or controlling, but it is helpful to refer to similar and common lists to check the boxes for ideas. Standards can give us a loose accountability as we prepare our students for whatever path they may choose to follow and to help us provide a transcript if needed.

Often it is helpful to view academics with a three-fold mindset and approach. Naturally, we consider the curriculum first and foremost. Not only is it key to find a curriculum that meets comprehensive academic content and standards, but it is also helpful to consider whether our choices fit our children's learning needs and styles. Be careful to not use academic standards as your sole direction while choosing a curriculum. The standards are not set up with individual students in mind but are universal.

Find the best resources to coordinate with the required standards and lay out your objectives, both in step and out of the box, for your children. Academic standards can be most intimidating as your children enter their middle to junior/high school years. This is most commonly when homeschooling families begin to question their styles, approach, content, success, or deficiencies.

## LIFE SKILLS

Obviously, we want to gauge our children and their abilities individually as they grow. What may work for one family or even one child in a family, may not work at the same pace for another. Life skills are incremental and can be easily added into developmental stages and ages as part of your homeschooling days. You will find printable checklists online to track your child's abilities and skill levels and to monitor their progress year to year. I think these standards and checklists are wonderful, but these are only a guide. Keep your child in mind when tracking and checking skills and progress. The value of homeschooling is to teach and train our children in their academics, but let's not forget the value of skills they use when they are in the public arena, with their peers, serving in ministry, applying for jobs, leaving for college—and let's not forget taking care of themselves independently year by year. As managers of our home, we don't have to be dictators, but careful teachers to train our children into their fullest potential. I like to encourage moms to think about their children as adults and those things they need to know, be able to do and manage on their home without you by their side. From a young age you can begin teaching your children the value of good work and responsibility.

*Teaching the worth of work and responsibility*
*is woven into the DNA of your homeschool day.*

Begin with the big picture and work backward in your approach to teaching your children ownership and the life skills they will need someday. At a young age, use concepts, words, and relatable life situations to help instill principles of good work. Make space in your morning routines for teamwork and excitement over a new "job." Do these chores together, modeling thoroughness and positivity. Implement independence with their personal routines, creativity, and their play spaces, and follow up with praise and affirmation that acknowledges the skill and responsibility they have worked hard for. From showing initiative to learning a new chore, skills are taught and not caught.

Often, we are leery of putting "too much" on our children at a young age. Because we know they will have a lifetime of work and challenges, we want them to enjoy their childhood and make positive memories, unburdened by the cares of this world. Friends, this mindset leaves room for a gap in the formative developmental years in their brain and their ideas and understanding of roles in the home, ownership, stewardship, and work ethic. These formative principles are the pillars to valuing work. When you wait to teach them life skills you leave space for pushback, entitlement, and more serious issues with time management as their academic workload picks up and they have never learned how to manage both.

**Basic Life Skill Concepts**

| | |
|---|---|
| Personal hygiene habits | Laziness vs. apathy |
| Personal space management | Helpfulness |
| Awareness of surroundings | Initiative |
| Verbal responses and ownership | Communication |
| Accountability | Time management |
| Authority | Life skills in the home |
| Neatness | Life skills in public |
| Productivity | Chores |

Remember, these are incremental, meaning they begin when our children are young and are gradually added or intentionally taught. Don't wait until you think your children are ready. We were made to work, serve one another, and bring glory to God. Our heart attitudes while teaching our children are just as vital as what we teach them.

Approach these tasks as unto the Lord, remembering your chief goal is to raise adults who love the Lord and serve Him and others. Weave their life skills into the motions of your day, teaching your children to live simultaneously with the actions and their learning. Life skills can be woven into your homeschooling every day. Time is often our biggest mental excuse and barrier.

## RELATIONSHIPS

If there is any indication of "how" socialized your child is as a homeschooler, the proof will show up at your school table every day. We may feel the peace of knowing our children are "away from the noise and outside influence" as we homeschool them. As true as this is, the protective nature may foster a lack of attention to their relational skills with others and the value of work in relationships outside the home. Our relationships in the home are indicative of the relationships our children will expect and have outside the home and school.

While working together during your homeschool, regularly take a few days to assess the interactions in your family: words, actions, attitudes, and responses to one another. This will give you an accurate view on the work you can begin implementing into your home and homeschool. Homeschooling can test the relationships in your home. Consider how spending 24/7 together can affect and form these interactions.

Some may say homeschooling relationships are not a true test of relationships in real life because we don't spend that many hours with anyone else. In reality, it is the best place to reveal how we value others and the dynamics we need to practice in our closest relationships. This the where the "rubber meets the road." We can begin using our school hours to practice the little steps to tolerance, patience, kindness, helpfulness, respect, and communication.

*If our children cannot love those at home,*
*how will they ever love others well?*

Relationship Checkboxes in Your Homeschool

1. Tolerating or managing noise levels with tolerance and patient communication
2. Self-control in words, responses, and reactions
3. Patience in waiting
4. Celebrating the success of others
5. Respect of others' space and time
6. Respect of others' property
7. Communication skills
8. Conflict resolution skills
9. Sensitivity to struggles, differences, and inconveniences
10. Deference

Obviously, perfection is not the goal, nor the standard, as we are all works in progress. Christ is our example and gives us His Word to guide and help us in all our relationships and the work of showing love where it is more difficult carefully and lovingly. With His help, and the daily work in the homeschool hours we have together with our children, we have what we need to prepare and foster good and godly relationships in our children, at home and beyond the walls of our home.

## CHARACTER

If you want to shake off the burden of "getting it right," then ask Jesus who *He* wants your child to be. This isn't a spiritual cliché to release or excuse the weight of the work and the investment you have before you. Raising and homeschooling our children with character and virtue is our goal, while educating and preparing them for a life of service and work. Turning to the written Word every day will guide us through the "put off and put on" process and point us to the virtues we can live by.

With the Holy Spirit's intercession, prayer, and application, our efforts are not only not in vain, but we have a hidden support system we can put all our hope in. Jesus doesn't expect us to be the only teacher of our children's heart. He takes our efforts and multiplies them in the sanctifying work He does in the spiritual disciplines we have helped our children learn. He speaks to them in their quiet time. He molds them in their time in the Word. He changes them in prayer and humility.

We are not only the teachers, but we are also on this journey with our children. The best teacher is growth. We are never left empty-handed when we have Jesus as the cornerstone of our home. Virtue and character are the deepest places that help guide our children's education to where the Lord leads them.

*All the academics in the world will mean nothing*
*without a virtuous and a holy purpose-filled life.*

Character and virtue are not a one and done deal. In the process of crafting an arrow, the longest and most tedious step is carefully placing the feathers with precision. The process of precision affects the way it turns and the way it's going to go when it's released from the bow. Even more significantly, the crafting of an arrow involves drying time. While teaching and modeling character in our homes, we need to remember and remind ourselves that it takes time.

*"For this very reason, make every effort to supplement your faith with virtue, and virtue with knowledge, and knowledge with self-control, and self-control with steadfastness, and steadfastness with godliness, and godliness with brotherly affection, and brotherly affection with love. For if these qualities are yours and are increasing, they keep you from being ineffective or unfruitful in the knowledge of our Lord Jesus Christ."* 2 Peter 1:5–8

Character takes time and is formative. Each step affects how the arrow (your child) is going to fly as soon as we let it go. Responsibility, attentiveness, honesty, ownership, accountability, integrity . . . finding the grace and remembering the careful balance of teaching and waiting.

*Weave virtue into the DNA of your homeschool and when it is time to launch your arrows, they will be prepared.*

*· · · · · · · personal reflection · · · · · · ·*

Where did my list of homeschooling checkboxes come from? Do my children see me changing and growing with them? What does God's Word say about the expectations in my homeschooling? Do my children know the verses these expectations are built on and why we have chosen the "checklists" we have?

*· · · · · · · personal challenge · · · · · · ·*

When I feel overwhelmed with the pressure of checking all the boxes, I will return to my purpose in raising a well-rounded, responsible adult who loves the Lord and not allow my head and heart to be distracted by comparison and the expectations of others.

*· · · · · · · drawing from the well · · · · · · ·*

Weariness often comes from worry. Our minutes spent in fear or control can be spent in prayer and petition. The man-made checklists are rubble in light of eternity.

> "A good name is to be chosen rather than great riches,
> and favor is better than silver or gold.
> The rich and the poor meet;
> the LORD is the Maker of them all.
> The prudent sees danger and hides himself,
> but the simple go on and suffer for it.
> The reward for humility and fear of the LORD
> is riches and honor and life.
> Thorns and snares are in the way of the crooked;
> whoever guards his soul will keep far from them.
> Train up a child in the way he should go;
> even when he is old he will not depart from it."
> Proverbs 22:1–6

*"Be very careful, then, how you live—not as unwise but as wise, making the most of every opportunity, because the days are evil."*
Ephesians 5:15–16 NIV

*"Let us not become weary in doing good, for at the proper time we will reap a harvest if we do not give up."* Galatians 6:9 NIV

*"Work willingly at whatever you do, as though you were working for the Lord rather than for people."* Colossians 3:23 NLT

•••• *a prayer for my homeschool* ••••

Father, I surrender any comparison or pressure of success I am putting on myself or on my children in our homeschool. Help me stay focused on the most valuable things. I want my children to see and know Your steadfast love in my life and in our home. Help me live Your principles and love out to them and to the world, so our homeschool is an overflow of Your presence in our lives. Guard my wayward heart from comparison and help me be diligent in homeschooling well. In Jesus' name, Amen.

*chapter 21*

- - • • • • • • • • • • • •

# The Joy of Capture
# and Release

$\mathcal{W}$e are never truly prepared for the day our children leave and take the next steps in their lives. All along, we knew this moment was coming, but how could we fathom the work it would take for us to do this well? The release is a rush of memories we have collected for almost two decades, and our hearts are barely able to process the emotions fast enough. We don't need more time; we need more bravery and strength to let go.

Everyone is celebrating the momentous occasion of your child's accomplishments. Those gold star moments you tenderly and lovingly cultivated in your homeschool have now culminated in one big celebration . . . but now you are only the observer of all that God has so faithfully done with your obedience and offering. You were faithful to the end. Be encouraged by one of my favorite analogies below. I couldn't have said this any better.

There comes a time —many times, actually—in the lives of our children where we have to put the basket in the water. We have to let go and trust the plan of the Father. The world is a scary place—a place where we fear our children could drown. But we must remember that we have to let go so that God can draw them from the waters for His great purpose. He has called us to be their parents, but they were His first.

My friend, whatever water you may be getting ready to put your basket into—remember that you have to put them in the water for God to draw them out and place them into His perfect plan. Though you might not be physically present with your child as much during the next phase of life, you can always petition the heart of the Father on their behalf.[4]

In all the moments you have invested into homeschooling your child, you have also been weaving that basket. Every fiber of your being has been woven into their heart and mind. Just as you have diligently worked to capture every moment, it is now time to let go and release them to the purpose God has called them to. While you have been working and sacrificing so much, you have also been building lifelong memories.

In your heart and mind, you hold their victories in the hardest learning struggles, their accomplishments, spiritual growth, and the spaces and places they had to overcome. You have wiped tears over pencil grips, washing dishes, and telling lies. You have learned hundreds of memory verses with them, stayed up late to learn their

4. Ashlei Woods, "Putting the Basket in the Water, Trusting God in the Next Phase of Your Child's Life," Bridge Christian Church, July 5, 2016, https://bridgechristian.wordpress.com/2016/07/05/putting-the-basket-in-the-water-trusting-god-in-the-next-phase-of-your-childs-life.

algebra lesson, corrected grammar and punctuation until your eyes were burning, and made over a thousand meals (or more if you do the math)—and every moment you have captured. They are memories you will have forever, and the impact those years and those moments had on them have not lost their power on you. Homeschooling your children has changed you. Homeschooling has made you stronger, better, smarter, and more versatile. The true meaning of sacrifice and surrender was not lost on your life.

The release is as much about you as them. They will take all the knowledge, skill, virtue, and purpose you have instilled in them with the help of the Holy Spirit and will live a life of purpose you cannot even imagine. Trust the process and the purpose God gave *you* when you said yes to homeschooling.

*When it is time to release your children, your journey*
*will be an inward and quiet processing of everything*
*you have captured over the years.*

The incredible journey to this point has given you the front row seat to your child's potential. You know the intricacies woven into who they were and are and will become. You understand how they think and how they learn. You can predict where they will struggle and could potentially keep them from falling or failing or even flailing. But friends, lean in close right here and hear my heart and trust my tried-and-true experience.

*You do not know what God wants to do with your*
*child's life—even when you know everything about them.*

Homeschooling is a calling, a privilege, and a sacrifice. But we cannot replace the inner work and calling God has on our children's lives. We must quiet our voices, step out of the way, and remember (although we will still have many more teachable moments with our children) that God's call on their life must be louder and bigger than our voices or opinions.

## TRUST AND TIMING

Homeschooling has always been on our timing and our terms. As our children get closer to graduation everything changes and shifts. Schedules become busier, opportunities cannot be missed, and the work intensifies. Despite the varying in a child's interests or pursuits, we still have the responsibility to help our children finish strong. Urgency feels great when we reach this point in homeschooling—the urgency to write or add more to their transcripts, to teach those last-minute life skills, and to be sure they know what they want to do next.

The world puts a lot of pressure on teens to make long-term decisions and plans before they graduate. We feel the pressure to send our kids off to learn from an institution when their peers set sail. There is nothing wrong with higher learning or tracking academically with peers and the natural progression in life for independence and growth. Our children need to make decisions and live out everything we have been teaching them with that goal in mind. Where we might feel the conflict is when our children are unsure, unready, or stuck in indecision. Timing is everything, and your child's pace can be set with multiple variables in mind.

Trust the process you began and allow the timing to speak for itself. Your work has not been in vain, so when the time comes, don't fall into the trap of worry or fear in the face of indecision, pressure, or timelines. If you have come this far, enjoy the end of the journey. Your faithfulness will reap rewards you may miss if your vision remains near-sighted. Step back and capture every last-minute moment.

*Your child's timeline and yours are not running at the same pace, and a new level of trust in what you have already taught them and how the Lord will lead them will be your constant as you pull them to the end—with joy.*

Below, you will find the solid truth statements and helpful ideas I preached to myself as I reached the finish line of release. Mark those that stand out to you and make note of them to remember all you have done so far.

### Truths & Helps

- Remind your child there is no urgency in true success.
- Speak confidence in the journey and abilities you see in your child.
- Begin early with discussions and options; explaining that a pivot is always an option.
- Trust the process and keep the momentum going.
- Remember, some children will launch fast and confidently and some take the slow start.

- Don't wait until the last minute to "fit everything in."
- Pace your life with the last years; not everyone can do everything when you are finishing strong.
- Pair their goals and needs with their assignments and schedules; eliminate the extra.
- Not all students will attend college, and if they do, it may not be at the same time as their peers.

Some students may not track with their peers, and the pressure may instigate a new level of insecurity and doubt for you both. Other students graduate early and know what they are doing and where they are going right out of the gate. You may feel as if you cannot keep up with them and worry the timing is premature. There will always be external voices to our child's pace and progress, their choices, and their future.

## RELATIONSHIP SHIFT

Your relationship will begin to transition from being the primary helper and teacher to releasing them into adulthood. This is one of the hardest lessons in raising kids for those who homeschool their children. We are learning to shift our time and expectations to releasing them and watching them own those areas for themselves. The dichotomy of raising kids to let them go is brutal and joyful at the same time. We are sad to let them go, yet so proud, happy, worried, and confident. Over the conflicted emotions and even confusion we are feeling we put on a brave face, continue to finish strong, and enjoy the moments all at the same time.

*Your relationship with your child will begin to shift and,*
*as hard as it is, this is the plan and was from the beginning.*
*God didn't give us our children to love, educate, and keep*
*to ourselves. Their purpose is His plan, and we are not*
*releasing them to the world, but into His care and call.*

Here are some defining markers you will recognize as normal, yet will feel are altogether difficult and different from the previous routine:

- Your children's plans will not always include you and will often be made without you in mind.
- They will be away from home more than they are present.
- Their interests may begin to shift and blindside *your* plans for their future.
- Apathy may begin to set in with academics and you may have to pull them to the end.
- Social life balance with academics will take on a life of its own.
- You may not be their trusted confidant in this season; they may stop sharing openly and freely like they once did; don't stop talking to them even when this is the new reality.
- Someone or something else will begin to replace you for affection and time; it is not personal, but it will feel that way.
- You may feel resistance to the ideas and schedules you've had in place for a long time.
- Someone else's voice may become louder than yours; be careful of the voices they are exposed to.

You have been your child's primary teacher, and the shift out of this role will afford you more free time. Don't forget to prepare your child ahead of time for the inevitable changes they too will face: from the space and time you will begin to spend away from one another to learning under a new style and environment of teaching and learning. This shift is often an area overlooked and can potentially be more challenging for your child than the natural flow of changes in other relationships. Begin this process in steps before it is time to launch them. The homeschooling student should learn adaptability, new environments, accountability to other adults in an educational environment, assignment ownership, and pivoting as needed.

This season is going to be hard no matter what. You cannot prepare your hearts for the changes in your relationships because this is a matter of growth and heart work, but you can help your child prepare for the academic or life changes ahead, because those are habit- or practice-forming. Joining a co-op or taking online or in-person college courses in their later years of high school before they choose their next steps will aid them in a few of the most predictable areas of change and stress they will experience.

The heart changes are inevitable, and most students will not be aware of those changes until they are years down the road. They don't understand the pull you are feeling even now as you see them growing and changing. You begin thinking about them leaving years in advance, and they are barely thinking about tomorrow. Their time and attention are directed to outward experiences and your focus is preparing them for what is next. This is where you will feel the strain. You may feel as if they are not "taking this seriously," or "putting in the time they need," or "spending quality time with family because these are your last memories with them."

As a parent, it will be helpful for you to separate their life choices or academic future from your relationship when you feel or think all those things. Your child is not choosing to act or not feel what you are feeling because they love you less or do not care. They are just growing up, and part of growing up is making or finding those lifelong friends, gaining more freedoms, and learning how to manage their time. Their inattentiveness is not about us.

As their homeschooling teacher, you will be careful to teach them responsibility and time management, paired with good grades and showing up to complete the "next steps," as part of their time management with social activities, family, and ministry. This has always been the most difficult space for me. I have learned the fine balance as a mom and the heartstrings attached to watching and feeling the pull and changes in our relationship; but stepping in the role of academic counselor (as their mom) and helping them prepare, guiding them in their choices, and taking those steps has proved to be the most difficult.

Our children know us as mom, and this counsel and guidance is heard as "mom advice," or a checklist we are giving them. This is where the relationship of letting go feels so personal. We have given our lives to teaching our children all of their days, and we know what is coming and the steps they need to do to get there; yet it is this space that feels like the biggest tug of war, and it certainly feels very personal because we love them and want the best for them.

Here are a few areas I have found helpful as a parent in this season of letting go:

- Ground your peace in their future in God's promises.
- Lean into the wisdom and input from various trusted voices and include your child in those conversations.
- Avoid overly emotional responses that center around your own feelings only.
- Ask the Lord for wisdom in the release.
- Let your children see your joy in the whole journey: tell them what you've loved about homeschooling; show them where they can practice and use what they have learned; and as the days get closer to their launch, speak joy and not fear.
- Change your relationship status from teacher to supporter and encourager.
- Love them like an adult now.
- Avoid guilt trips or emotional power struggles to coerce them into spending more time with you.
- Show your children you are not codependent on them and give them permission to leave with confidence and excitement.

## HOLD ON AND LET GO

Finishing the race with joy will be your choice. There would be nothing worse than finishing with only regret. Each moment matters right now. Every paragraph rewritten, math problem corrected, sports games attended, music lessons, college application, gripping the wheel while they learned how to drive, first year of school pictures and academic transcripts completed . . . these are the moments you hold on to while letting go.

God's purpose in calling you to homeschool is just beginning. While it feels like the end, this is truly just the start of the biggest and most beautiful picture you can imagine. Your investment and their hard work, paired with God's divine purpose will unfold before your eyes as you step back and watch and wait. There will always be pieces of you that walk out the door when your homeschooling journey is over. Trust me when I tell you how God fills in those gaps with new and amazing ideas and opportunities— and even better, He never leaves you or forsakes you.

Don't be afraid to allow your children to grow beyond their spaces and to feel discomfort in new places. I have witnessed homeschooled, first-year college students with the physical inability to attend college, take tests, live away from home, or make small, and therefore, big decisions. Be careful not to fall into the homeschooling codependent patterns. Don't wait until the last two years to identify small symptoms of this pattern that can make the letting go harder for them and easier for us.

*Part of the homeschooling journey is the preparation of letting go. It doesn't just happen. It will require intentional steps, new habits in your homeschooling, and a dependency on God to hold your child in His grip. Your heart will be okay.*

Here are areas I've found helpful in preparing my child for the "release":

- Implement life goals or future academic steps in progression.
- Identify academic areas in which your child needs more work to be prepared for whatever future steps they may choose.

- Instill practices of time management.
- Teach good study habits; homeschooling may create a "teacher-led" pattern.
- Schedule regular family meetings about change and family patterns you would like to keep the same and discuss areas of growth; this helps everyone identify the feelings they experience as the changes take place.
- Have your students try new and hard things in their last years before the big launch (e.g., camps, college classes, internships, filling out forms, service opportunities).
- Begin teaching financial responsibility and stewardship.
- Set up boundaries for behavior for each child because when social schedules change, the newfound freedom takes everyone by surprise and sometimes academics or life balance suffers.
- Speak truth and confidence into and over your child's life.
- Give your child the tools and life habits to step into unknown spaces.
- Train your children how to communicate and speak to adults.
- Create opportunities for them to make small and big decisions and guide them through it.
- Homeschool your child in academics, and don't skip out on social adaptation.
- Allow room for them to grow and to fail—making mistakes and finding solutions is a life lesson they have to learn for themselves.

## THE JOY FACTOR

Joy is a mysterious thing. We set high expectations on what we think we should feel or experience in the joy of our homeschooling. The idea to finish with joy on any given day can seem almost impossible, let alone the whole journey. When I consider all the years I have been homeschooling and launching my children into their next seasons, the "joy" moments are what I hold the dearest.

Homeschooling with joy is to capture the moments of progress—to teach the Word and watch them live it out and to see milestones reached. Homeschooling with joy is to grow in the most difficult places and put our confidence in the foundation we have laid with God's sustaining grace.

*........ personal reflection ........*

I homeschool with joy when I see a job well done.

I homeschool with joy when I feel the sacrifice and don't feel like a martyr.

I homeschool with joy when I hear my children laugh and love learning.

I homeschool with joy when I see my children take initiative for the now and the future.

I homeschool with joy when things are hard because I hold on to the promises of His faithfulness in my perseverance.

I homeschool with joy because I am not waiting for it to be easy.

I homeschool with joy because I am my child's teacher and I have been entrusted with His plan.

I homeschool with joy because I don't need to feel happy and excited when it is so very hard, but joy in knowing there will be new mercies every morning.

I homeschool with joy because God called me to this, and He is the author and finisher of my faith.

I homeschool with joy, so my children do not begrudge the example I set for them.

I homeschool with joy because I choose joy.

*........ personal challenge ........*

When I choose joy in my homeschooling, it doesn't negate the hard and difficult days.

When I choose joy in my homeschooling, it is not a pretense or a covering of all things wrong and a blank canvas for my children to do whatever they would like.

When I choose joy in my homeschooling, I am choosing an attitude of joy in knowing some things are out of my control.

When I choose joy in my homeschooling, I have learned to separate the love I have for my children from the conflicts I face, and I remember again why I said yes to the journey.

When I choose joy in my homeschooling, I have learned to find motivators not contingent on control or perfection.

When I choose joy in homeschooling, I remember I am never alone in this.

When I choose joy in homeschooling, I remember God's faithfulness and how far we've come.

When I choose joy in homeschooling, I remind myself where true joy is found and there is absolutely no way I could fabricate or feel true joy without the love of Jesus and the hope He can give me.

······· *drawing from the well* ·······

When I choose to finish homeschooling with joy, I remember God has promised us we will reap a harvest when we do not give up. When I choose to finish with joy, I relinquish my "rights" to receive the glory and remember it was Him who began a good work in us and will be faithful to complete it.

God's Word reminds us how to finish with joy. Write the verses below in your homeschool planner and keep them before you as a reminder to not grow weary.

This verse has encouraged me to stay the course and not grow weary while doing so:

> *"Let us not become weary in doing good, for at the proper time we will reap a harvest if we do not give up."* Galatians 6:9 NIV

This was Paul's prayer for the Romans:

*"May the God of hope fill you with all joy and peace in believing,*
*so that by the power of the Holy Spirit you may abound in hope."*
Romans 15:13

This is the joy the psalmist had in the presence of God:

*"You make known to me the path of life; in your presence there is*
*fullness of joy; at your right hand are pleasures forevermore."*
Psalm 16:11

•••• *a prayer for my homeschool* ••••

Father God, some of us feel like we are limping to the finish line, and some are running with the baton ready to pass it to the next season like they are ready for the gold medal. Wherever we are and however we feel, we want to give the glory to You. We can see the finish line before us and we desire to finish strong. Show us, guide us, and give us strength to persevere, to remember You have gone before us and we have come too far to grow weary and give up now. You have given us wisdom, direction, and sustained us for the long haul. We see flourishing before us and as much as we know we had a part in this, we want to praise *You* for being the author and finisher of our faith. Help us to make it to the finish line, arm in arm with our children. Thank You for this amazing privilege to raise children in Your Word and to capture their moments of growth along the way. We give them to You again Lord. To You be the glory forever. Amen.

# Acknowledgments

A homeschool is only as strong as the hope it finds in Jesus. From the very start, He has been my portion and my steadfast strength. To Jesus, all my faith and hope to finish well, I give to you.

To Jess Herberger, for giving me the nudge to be brave. Your words and prayers carried me through every page. Thank you for your words, "I am proud of you." You know the value and impact those five words have on me. Your writing wisdom is beyond words on a page. Thank you for believing in me.

Amanda Cleary Eastep, your detailed work and edits brought this book to life. You were careful with my "heart words," and yet called me to be a better writer. For this, I am so grateful. Your work is brilliant.

Catherine Parks, you are the most amazing listener. As the vision for this book evolved, changed, and went back to the drawing board on numerous occasions, your labor of love and gentle guidance to the final product was unparalleled. Thank you for inviting me to coffee. I am grateful I said yes.

Dan, you have always been in my corner, reminding me I was called to write this book. You never let me doubt our homeschooling, even when I felt like I was failing at every turn. There you were, at every corner, reminding me to stay the course and to finish strong. Thank you for trusting me to teach our children. Our life is marked by sacrifice and love. Your imprint is on every page.

Ben, Sarah, Matthew, Leah, Lydia, Eden, Samuel, Maryahna, Ava, and Audrey, you have taught me so much. Our homeschool journey has had its highs and lows, but the One who held us all together when we weren't sure if we were going to make it, still holds us all today. You changed me and taught me to hold on to hope, right to the end. You are on every page, teaching us to remember that every child is different. This is your story as much as mine. I am passing this baton to you now. You are ready.